NOTE

1. All recipes serve four unless otherwise stated.

2. All spoon measurements are level.

3. All eggs are sizes 3 or 4 unless otherwise stated.

4. Preparation times given are an average calculated during recipe testing.

5. Metric and imperial measurements have been calculated separately. Use one set of measurements only as they are not exact equivalents.

6. Cooking times may vary slightly depending on the individual oven. Dishes should be placed in the centre of the oven unless otherwise specified.

7. Always preheat the oven or grill to the specified temperature.

8. Spoon measures can be bought in both imperial and metric sizes to give accurate measurement of small quantities.

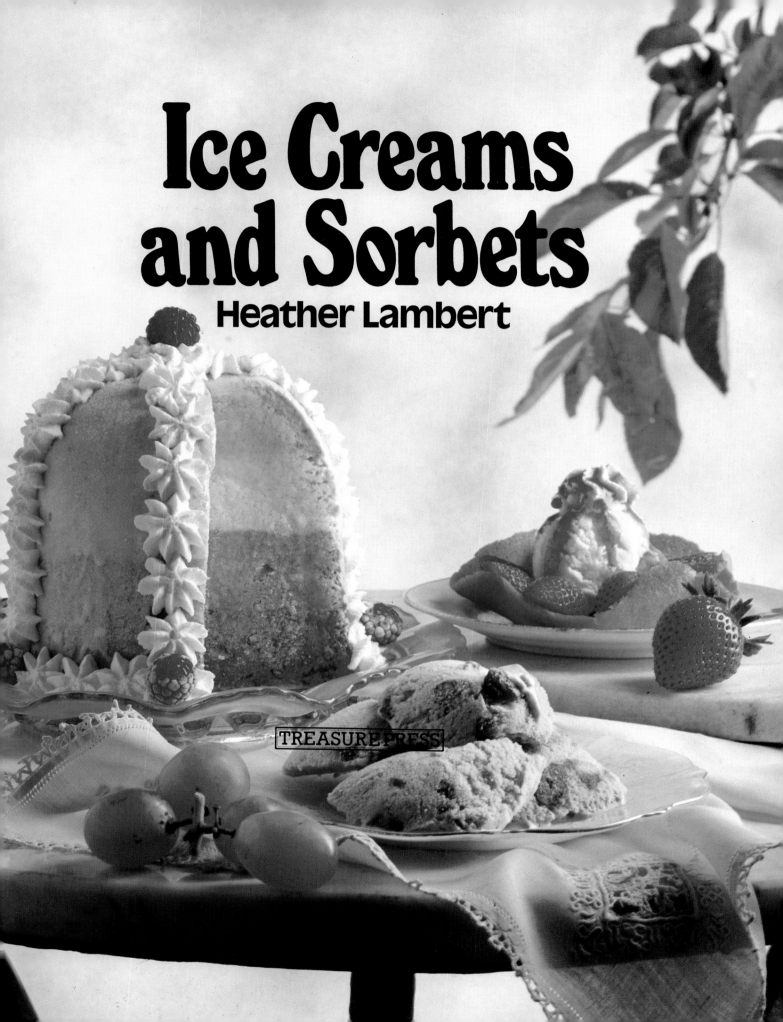

Ice Creams and Sorbets

Heather Lambert

TREASURE PRESS

Contents

First published in Great Britain in 1982 by
Octopus Books Limited under the title,
Ice Creams

This edition published in 1985 by
Treasure Press
59 Grosvenor Street
London W1

© 1982 Hennerwood Publications Limited

ISBN 1 85051 071 7

Printed in Hong Kong

INTRODUCTION

There seems little doubt that ice creams originated in China, where they were being made as long ago as 3000 B.C. As contact with the East developed, the secrets of ice cream preparation gradually spread to Europe. The Romans prepared water ices and various iced sweets, and it seems likely that ice cream-making methods spread from Italy into France in the 16th century. By the reign of Charles I, ices had become a fashionable delicacy at the English court. In those days, ice for freezing ice creams was collected in winter and stored with layers of salt in 'ice houses', which were usually deep pits in the ground covered with straw and turf.

By the 19th century, ice cream eating had become widespread and ices were sold from booths at street corners in small glass dishes. Known as 'hokey pokeys', these ice creams were the forerunners of modern ice cream cornets. European immigrants then introduced ice cream to America, where the ice cream sundae and the ice cream parlour were invented. It was there, too, that ice cream first began to be produced commercially on a large scale.

Before the invention of the refrigerator and freezer, however, ice cream-making was a lengthy and tedious process which only the wealthy could afford. The ice cream was frozen in churns lined with crushed ice and salt. A metal bowl of mixture was placed in the churn and covered with a lid fitted with a paddle which could be turned by a handle. The paddle then had to be worked by hand to prevent the mixture crystallizing as it froze. The finished ice cream could be stored for a short time in a box thickly lined with salted ice.

Despite these difficulties, chefs all over Europe vied with each other to produce more and more elaborate confections, often making ice cream bombes by freezing layers of various flavours inside decorative moulds. In the latter part of the 19th century, a cookery school was opened in London where ladies could attend with their cooks to learn the art of producing such delicacies.

Ice cream-making machines

Modern methods of refrigeration have made ice cream-making far simpler. However, electric ice cream-making machines for the home work on the same principle as the old-fashioned churns. The mixture to be frozen is placed in a circular metal container which fits round a small electric motor. Paddles are placed in the container and fitted to the motor, then a lid is put on and the machine is put in the coldest part of the freezer and switched on. The paddles swing round gently and automatically rise when the mixture comes close to freezing point. The ice cream can then be left in the container to finish freezing, or removed to a freezer container to free the machine for making other ices.

The recipes given in this book are for making ices without the aid of such a machine, but if you do own one it will save the extra work of beating the ice creams to prevent crystallization during the freezing process. When a recipe gives instructions to freeze until the mixture is of a mushy consistency before folding in cream or egg whites, the machine must be watched carefully to ensure that the mixture does not harden too much. When the whipped ingredients have been folded in, the mixture may either be returned to the machine or placed in a freezer container and completed according to the recipe.

Freezing and storing ice cream

The faster ice cream can be frozen, the better the result. Always place the mixture to be frozen in the coldest part of the freezer. If your freezer has a fast-freeze compartment, it is wise to have the compartment virtually empty so that the mixture can rest on the base, which is the coldest section. Do not attempt to freeze too many mixtures at any one time, as the bulk of food will raise the temperature of the freezer and slow down the freezing process. If you have an override switch on your freezer thermostat, turn this on for the duration of the freezing process.

Many of these recipes recommend beating the mixture several times during the first few hours of freezing. The best way of doing this is to use a freezer container which allows enough room to beat the mixture in the container, rather than transferring it to a bowl, which slows down the freezing process. Use a wooden spoon and beat the mixture for about $\frac{1}{2}$ minute each time. This makes the ice cream light and creamy and prevents any crystals forming.

Once completed, it is important to store your ice creams in well-sealed freezer containers. This prevents them from taking up the flavours of other foods being stored and avoids evaporation occurring. Rigid plastic or polythene containers are the most successful kind to use. Storage time depends very much on the variety of the ice cream and there are no hard-and-fast rules that can be given. Most ice creams need at least 3–4 hours' total freezing time and home-made ice creams are best eaten within 3 months of preparation. If stored for longer, the texture and flavour will begin to deteriorate.

Economical hints

Making ice cream is an excellent way of using up excess soft fruits during the summer months, especially as the fruits need not be perfect. If you have a large family, or are planning some entertaining, you could take advantage of the 'pick-your-own' centres which offer a large variety of seasonal fruits and can be found all over the country within easy reach of most towns and villages.

When making a custard-based ice cream, it is sensible to prepare a sorbet or a meringue cake at the same time to prevent wasting the egg whites. Alternatively, the whites may be stored in the freezer for use at a later date. When using egg whites that have been frozen in any quantity, leave them to defrost and then measure them out, allowing 25 ml/ 1 fl oz to represent 1 egg white.

Why home-made?

Home-made ice creams are well worth the effort and expense to prepare. Ingredients such as eggs, cream, yogurt and fresh fruits produce quite different flavours and textures to commercially bought ice creams and even the simplest of home-made ice creams tastes special.

Serving ice cream

Different recipes and quantities will affect the time ice cream takes to defrost but generally home-made ice cream is served at its best if removed from the freezer to the refrigerator for about 45 minutes before serving. It will then be at the correct consistency to form neat scoops or spoonfuls. This is particularly important when using it to fill meringue cases or coupelles. Many recipe books suggest you remove ice cream from the freezer and leave it on one side for 15–20 minutes before serving, but if the kitchen is too warm the ice cream will soon begin to melt on the outside. The longer period in the refrigerator is found to be more successful.

Successful sugar boiling

Three stages of sugar boiling are used in this book. It is difficult to give an indication of the time each one takes and the easiest way to accurately identify each of the stages is to use a sugar thermometer. Below are the temperatures for each stage, and quick, alternative tests which can be used, if a thermometer is not available.

Smooth stage (for syrups)
102°–104°C, 214°–218°F
Dip a spoon into the syrup and allow it to cool for a moment or two. Rub a little syrup between the thumb and forefinger. The fingers should slide smoothly but the syrup should cling to the skin.

Thread stage (for ice creams, sorbets and sauces)
110°–112°C, 230°–234°F
Using a small spoon remove a little of the syrup and allow it to fall from the spoon on to a dish. The syrup should form a fine, thin thread when the correct stage has been reached.

Soft ball stage (for sauces)
113°–118°C, 235°–245°F
Drop a little of the syrup into a cupful of cold water. The syrup should form a soft ball, which flattens when taken out of the water.

CUSTARD-BASED ICE CREAM Basic vanilla ice cream

Most of the custard-based ice creams use single cream. The result is deliciously smooth and rich, but it is an expensive way of making ice cream. Therefore some milk-based custard recipes have been included in this chapter, using an extra egg yolk to make a good thick base for whatever flavour is to be added.
The basic custard plays an important part in the success of custard-based ice creams. The mixture must never be allowed to boil, otherwise the eggs will scramble and the mixture will become coarse and lumpy.
Custard-based ice creams need at least 3–4 hours' total freezing time. During this time the ice cream is usually beaten a number of times at hourly intervals (see page 4).
These ice creams all benefit from being removed from the freezer to the refrigerator 45 minutes before serving to be of a perfect consistency.

Metric	*Imperial*
450 ml single cream	*15 fl oz single cream*
1 vanilla pod or 3–4 drops vanilla essence	*1 vanilla pod or 3–4 drops vanilla essence*
3 egg yolks	*3 egg yolks*
100 g caster sugar	*4 oz caster sugar*
150 ml double or whipping cream	*5 fl oz double or whipping cream*

Preparation time: 15–25 minutes, plus freezing
Cooking time: 25 minutes

If you use the vanilla essence instead of a vanilla pod the final flavour will be stronger.

To make a vanilla custard, put the single cream and the vanilla pod in a heavy-based saucepan and bring the mixture very slowly to boiling point. Remove from the heat, cover and allow to stand for 10 minutes. Remove the vanilla pod and reheat the cream to simmering point.
Alternatively, add the vanilla essence to the single cream and gently heat to simmering point.
Beat the egg yolks and sugar in a large bowl until thick and pale yellow in colour. Gradually pour the hot cream into the egg mixture, stirring constantly.
Strain the mixture into a heavy-based or double saucepan and stir over a gentle heat until the custard thickens enough to coat the back of a wooden spoon. Do not allow to boil. Pour into a large mixing bowl and allow the completed vanilla custard to go cold.
Beat the double or whipping cream until it forms soft peaks, then gently fold into the custard.
Pour into a freezer container and freeze. Beat the mixture twice, at hourly intervals. Cover, seal and freeze for at least a further 1–2 hours.
Serves 4–6

Cassata

Metric
1 quantity Basic Vanilla
  Ice Cream (page 8)
100 g crystallized fruits,
  chopped
2 × 15 ml spoons brandy
50 g unsalted mixed nuts,
  chopped
150 ml double or whipping
  cream, to serve

Imperial
1 quantity Basic Vanilla
  Ice Cream (page 8)
4 oz crystallized fruits,
  chopped
2 tablespoons brandy
2 oz unsalted mixed nuts,
  chopped
5 fl oz double or whipping
  cream, to serve

Preparation time: 30 minutes, plus defrosting, soaking and freezing
Cooking time: 5 minutes

Allow the basic vanilla ice cream to soften for about 1 hour in the refrigerator. Meanwhile put the chopped crystallized fruits in a small bowl, pour over the brandy and leave to soak for 1 hour.
Toast the chopped nuts gently under a preheated low grill, turning them with a fork to ensure even browning. Allow to cool.
Gently stir the fruits, brandy and nuts into the softened ice cream and spoon the mixture into a 15 cm/6 inch loose-based cake tin. Place the tin in a polythene bag, seal, and freeze.
To serve, turn out the cassata and decorate with rosettes of whipped cream, using a forcing bag fitted with a rose piping nozzle.
Serves 6–8

Pistachio ice cream

Metric
450 ml milk
1 vanilla pod or 2–3 drops
  vanilla essence
3 egg yolks
100 g caster sugar
150 ml double or whipping
  cream
50 g pistachio nuts,
  chopped

Imperial
¾ pint milk
1 vanilla pod or 2–3 drops
  vanilla essence
3 egg yolks
4 oz caster sugar
5 fl oz double or whipping
  cream
2 oz pistachio nuts,
  chopped

Preparation time: 20 minutes, plus freezing
Cooking time: 25 minutes

Use the milk, vanilla pod or vanilla essence, egg yolks and caster sugar to make a vanilla custard (see Basic Vanilla Ice Cream, page 8). Allow to cool, then pour the custard into a freezer container and freeze for about 1½ hours until mushy.
Beat the cream until it forms soft peaks. Gently fold the chopped nuts and cream into the frozen custard, and freeze. Beat the mixture three times, at hourly intervals. Cover, seal and freeze.
Serves 4–6

Basic vanilla ice cream with Russian cigar biscuits; Cassata; Pistachio ice cream

Chocolate and orange ice cream; Chestnut and chocolate ripple; Mocha ice cream; Rum and raisin ice cream

Chocolate and orange ice cream

Metric	Imperial
450 ml single cream	15 fl oz single cream
1 vanilla pod or 2–3 drops vanilla essence	1 vanilla pod or 2–3 drops vanilla essence
3 egg yolks	3 egg yolks
100 g caster sugar	4 oz caster sugar
75 g plain chocolate, broken into pieces	3 oz plain chocolate, broken into pieces
2 × 15 ml spoons Orange Curaçao	2 tablespoons Orange Curaçao
150 ml double or whipping cream	5 fl oz double or whipping cream
grated orange rind, to serve	grated orange rind, to serve

Preparation time: 25 minutes, plus freezing
Cooking time: 30 minutes

Use the single cream, vanilla pod or vanilla essence, egg yolks and caster sugar to make a vanilla custard (see Basic Vanilla Ice Cream, page 8). Pour into a large mixing bowl and allow to cool slightly.
Place the chocolate pieces in a small heatproof bowl. Melt the chocolate over a pan of gently simmering water, stirring as little as possible to avoid crystallization. Cool slightly, then stir into the warm custard with the Orange Curaçao. Allow to go cold.
Beat the double or whipping cream until it forms soft peaks and fold into the chocolate custard. Pour into a freezer container and freeze. Beat the mixture twice, at hourly intervals. Cover, seal and freeze.
Sprinkle with grated orange rind before serving.
Serves 4–6

Chestnut and chocolate ripple

Metric	Imperial
450 ml single cream	15 fl oz single cream
1 vanilla pod or 2–3 drops vanilla essence	1 vanilla pod or 2–3 drops vanilla essence
3 egg yolks	3 egg yolks
75 g caster sugar	3 oz caster sugar
1 × 200 g can unsweetened chestnut purée	1 × 7 oz can unsweetened chestnut purée
150 ml double or whipping cream	5 fl oz double or whipping cream
75 g plain chocolate, melted and almost cold	3 oz plain chocolate, melted and almost cold

Preparation time: 25 minutes, plus freezing
Cooking time: 30 minutes

Use the single cream, vanilla pod or vanilla essence, egg yolks and caster sugar to make a vanilla custard (see Basic Vanilla Ice Cream, page 8). Pour into a large mixing bowl and allow to go cold.
Stir in the chestnut purée. Beat the double or whipping cream until it forms soft peaks and fold into the chestnut mixture. Pour into a freezer container and freeze for about 1½ hours until mushy.
Gently beat the frozen mixture and then pour in the cooled chocolate and ripple it through with a fork. Cover, seal and freeze.
Serves 4–6

Mocha ice cream

Metric	**Imperial**
450 ml milk	¾ pint milk
1 vanilla pod or 2–3 drops vanilla essence	1 vanilla pod or 2–3 drops vanilla essence
4 egg yolks	4 egg yolks
75 g caster sugar	3 oz caster sugar
100 g plain chocolate, broken into pieces	4 oz plain chocolate, broken into pieces
1 × 5 ml spoon coffee dissolved in 1 × 15 ml spoon boiling water	1 teaspoon coffee dissolved in 1 tablespoon boiling water
150 ml double or whipping cream	5 fl oz double or whipping cream
chocolate curls, to serve	chocolate curls, to serve

Preparation time: 25 minutes, plus freezing
Cooking time: 30 minutes

This recipe uses milk instead of cream for the vanilla custard, making the ice cream cheaper and less rich.

Use the milk, vanilla pod or vanilla essence, egg yolks and caster sugar to make a vanilla custard (see Basic Vanilla Ice Cream, page 8). Pour into a large mixing bowl and allow to cool.
Put the chocolate in a small heatproof bowl with the coffee. Melt the chocolate over a pan of gently simmering water. Beat gently into the custard. Allow to go completely cold.
Beat the double or whipping cream until it forms soft peaks and fold into the custard mixture. Pour into a freezer container and freeze. Beat the mixture twice, at hourly intervals. Cover, seal and freeze.
Sprinkle with chocolate curls before serving.
Serves 4–6

Rum and raisin ice cream

Metric	**Imperial**
75 g seedless raisins	3 oz seedless raisins
4 × 15 ml spoons white rum	4 tablespoons white rum
450 ml single cream	15 fl oz single cream
1 vanilla pod or 2–3 drops vanilla essence	1 vanilla pod or 2–3 drops vanilla essence
3 egg yolks	3 egg yolks
100 g caster sugar	4 oz caster sugar
150 ml double or whipping cream	5 fl oz double or whipping cream

Preparation time: 25 minutes, plus freezing
Cooking time: 25 minutes

Put the rum and raisins in a small bowl and set aside to marinate. Meanwhile, use the single cream, vanilla pod or vanilla essence, egg yolks and caster sugar to make a vanilla custard (see Basic Vanilla Ice Cream, page 8). Pour into a large mixing bowl and allow to go cold.
Beat the double or whipping cream until it forms soft peaks and fold gently into the custard with the rum and raisins. Pour into a freezer container and freeze. Beat the mixture twice, at hourly intervals. Cover, seal and freeze.
Serves 4–6

Honey and lemon ice cream

Preparation time: 25 minutes, plus freezing
Cooking time: 25 minutes

Metric	*Imperial*
450 ml milk	*¾ pint milk*
2 strips lemon peel	*2 strips lemon peel*
4 egg yolks	*4 egg yolks*
75 g caster sugar	*3 oz caster sugar*
1 × 15 ml spoon clear honey	*1 tablespoon clear honey*
150 ml double or whipping cream	*5 fl oz double or whipping cream*
1 × 15 ml spoon grated lemon rind	*1 tablespoon grated lemon rind*

Put the milk and lemon peel in a heavy-based saucepan and gently bring to the boil. Remove from the heat, cover, and leave to infuse for 10 minutes. Remove the lemon peel and heat the lemon-flavoured milk to simmering point.

Beat the egg yolks and sugar together in a large mixing bowl until thick and pale yellow in colour. Gradually stir the hot milk into the egg mixture.

Strain the mixture into a heavy-based or double saucepan and stir over a gentle heat until the custard thickens enough to coat the back of a wooden spoon. Do not allow to boil. Pour into a large mixing bowl, stir in the honey and allow to go cold.

Beat the cream until it forms soft peaks and fold into the custard with the grated lemon rind. Pour into a freezer container and freeze. Beat the mixture twice, at hourly intervals. Cover, seal and freeze.

Serves 4–6

Black cherry ice cream

Metric
300 ml milk
3 egg yolks
100 g caster sugar
1 × 425 g can black
    cherries, drained
150 ml double or whipping
    cream

Imperial
½ pint milk
3 egg yolks
4 oz caster sugar
1 × 15 oz can black
    cherries, drained
5 fl oz double or whipping
    cream

Preparation time: 25 minutes, plus freezing
Cooking time: 15 minutes

Reserve the cherry juice from this recipe for making
Black Cherry Syrup (page 19).

Heat the milk to simmering point. Beat the egg yolks
and sugar together in a large mixing bowl until thick
and pale yellow in colour. Gradually pour the hot milk
into the egg mixture, stirring all the time.
Strain the mixture into a heavy-based or double
saucepan and stir over a gentle heat until the custard
thickens enough to coat the back of a wooden spoon.
Do not allow to boil. Allow to cool, then pour the
custard into a freezer container and freeze for about
1½ hours until mushy.
Remove the stones and finely chop the cherries. Beat
the cream until it forms soft peaks. Fold the cream
and the chopped cherries into the frozen custard, and
freeze. Beat the mixture three times, at hourly intervals. Cover, seal and freeze.
Serves 4–6

Prune ice cream

Metric
225 g prunes, soaked for
    4 hours in 150 ml water
1 × 5 cm cinnamon stick
450 ml single cream
3 egg yolks
100 g caster sugar
150 ml double or whipping
    cream

Imperial
8 oz prunes, soaked for
    4 hours in ¼ pint water
1 × 2 inch cinnamon stick
15 fl oz single cream
3 egg yolks
4 oz caster sugar
5 fl oz double or whipping
    cream

Preparation time: 30 minutes, plus soaking and
freezing
Cooking time: 25 minutes

Put the prunes, the soaking liquid and cinnamon stick
in a saucepan. Simmer over a gentle heat until the
prunes are soft. Discard the cinnamon stick and allow
to cool slightly.
Remove the stones from the prunes and liquidize
to a purée with their cooking juice. Allow to go cold.
Meanwhile, heat the single cream to simmering point.
Beat the egg yolks and sugar together in a large mixing
bowl until thick and pale yellow in colour. Gradually
pour the hot cream into the egg mixture, stirring all
the time.
Strain the mixture into a heavy-based or double
saucepan and stir over a gentle heat until the custard
thickens enough to coat the back of a wooden spoon.
Do not allow to boil. Pour into a large mixing bowl
and allow to go cold.
Stir in the prune purée. Beat the double or whipping
cream until it forms soft peaks, then fold into the
prune mixture. Pour into a freezer container and
freeze. Beat the mixture twice, at hourly intervals.
Cover, seal and freeze.
Serves 4–6

Honey and lemon ice cream; Black cherry ice cream;
Prune ice cream

Oatcake ice cream

Metric	Imperial
450 ml single cream	15 fl oz single cream
3 egg yolks	3 egg yolks
100 g soft brown sugar	4 oz soft brown sugar
100 g Scottish oatcakes	4 oz Scottish oatcakes
150 ml double or whipping cream	5 fl oz double or whipping cream
2 × 15 ml spoons whisky (optional)	2 tablespoons whisky (optional)

Preparation time: 20 minutes, plus freezing
Cooking time: 20 minutes

Heat the single cream to simmering point. Do not allow to boil. Beat the egg yolks and sugar together in a large mixing bowl until the mixture becomes thick and pale yellow in colour. Gradually pour the hot cream into the egg mixture, stirring all the time.
Strain the mixture into a heavy-based or double saucepan and stir over a gentle heat until the custard thickens enough to coat the back of a wooden spoon. Do not boil. Allow to cool, then pour the custard into a freezer container and freeze for about 1½ hours until mushy.
Toast the oatcakes slowly under a preheated low grill until crisp, then crush them finely with a rolling pin, or put them in a grinder. Allow to go cold.
Beat the double or whipping cream until it forms soft peaks. Fold the cream into the frozen custard together with the oatcake crumbs and the whisky, and freeze. Beat the mixture three times, at hourly intervals. Cover, seal and freeze.
Serves 4–6

Brown breadcrumb ice cream

Metric	Imperial
450 ml milk	¾ pint milk
1 vanilla pod or 2–3 drops vanilla essence	1 vanilla pod or 2–3 drops vanilla essence
4 egg yolks	4 egg yolks
100 g caster sugar	4 oz caster sugar
50 g dry brown breadcrumbs	2 oz dry brown breadcrumbs
150 ml double or whipping cream	5 fl oz double or whipping cream

Preparation time: 25 minutes, plus freezing
Cooking time: 30 minutes

Use the milk, vanilla pod or vanilla essence, egg yolks and caster sugar to make a vanilla custard (see Basic Vanilla Ice Cream, page 8). Allow to cool, then pour the custard into a freezer container and freeze for about 1½ hours until mushy.
Gently toast the brown breadcrumbs under a pre-heated low grill, turning them with a fork to ensure that they toast evenly. Set aside to cool.
Beat the cream until it forms soft peaks. Fold the cream and the breadcrumbs into the frozen custard, and freeze. Beat the mixture once after 1 hour, then cover, seal and freeze.
Serves 4–6

Ginger ice cream

Metric	*Imperial*
450 ml milk	¾ pint milk
1 × 5 ml spoon ground ginger	1 teaspoon ground ginger
4 egg yolks	4 egg yolks
75 g caster sugar	3 oz caster sugar
150 ml double or whipping cream	5 fl oz double or whipping cream
75 g crystallized or stem ginger, finely chopped	3 oz crystallized or stem ginger, finely chopped
25 g glacé cherries, chopped	1 oz glacé cherries, chopped

Preparation time: 20 minutes, plus freezing
Cooking time: 15 minutes

Put the milk and the ground ginger in a heavy-based saucepan and bring to simmering point. Beat the egg yolks and sugar together in a large mixing bowl until thick and pale yellow in colour. Gradually pour the hot milk into the egg mixture, stirring all the time. Strain the mixture into a heavy-based or double saucepan and stir over a gentle heat until the custard thickens enough to coat the back of a wooden spoon. Do not allow to boil. Pour into a large mixing bowl and allow to go cold.
Beat the cream until it forms soft peaks, then fold into the custard. Pour into a freezer container and freeze for 1 hour.
Beat the crystallized ginger and glacé cherries into the ice cream and return it to the freezer for a further hour. Beat again, then cover, seal and freeze.
Serves 4–6

Earl Grey ice cream

Metric	*Imperial*
450 ml milk	¾ pint milk
2 × 5 ml spoons Earl Grey tea	2 teaspoons Earl Grey tea
1 strip lemon peel	1 strip lemon peel
3 egg yolks	3 egg yolks
100 g caster sugar	4 oz caster sugar
150 ml double or whipping cream	5 fl oz double or whipping cream

Preparation time: 25 minutes, plus freezing
Cooking time: 25 minutes

Put the milk, tea and lemon peel in a heavy-based saucepan and gently bring to the boil. Remove from the heat, cover, and leave to infuse for 10 minutes. Strain, then reheat the tea-flavoured milk to simmering point.
Beat together the egg yolks and sugar in a large mixing bowl until thick and pale yellow in colour. Gradually stir the hot milk into the egg mixture.
Strain the mixture into a heavy-based or double saucepan and stir over a gentle heat until the custard thickens enough to coat the back of a wooden spoon. Do not allow to boil. Pour into a large mixing bowl and allow to go cold.
Beat the cream until it forms soft peaks and fold into the custard. Pour into a freezer container and freeze. Beat the mixture twice, at hourly intervals. Cover, seal and freeze.
Serves 4–6

Oatcake ice cream; Brown breadcrumb ice cream with ginger snap; Ginger ice cream; Earl Grey ice cream

Almond and Kirsch ice cream

Metric	Imperial
450 ml milk	¾ pint milk
1 vanilla pod or 2–3 drops vanilla essence	1 vanilla pod or 2–3 drops vanilla essence
3 egg yolks	3 egg yolks
100 g caster sugar	4 oz caster sugar
150 ml double or whipping cream	5 fl oz double or whipping cream
100 g whole almonds, chopped	4 oz whole almonds, chopped
2 × 15 ml spoons Kirsch	2 tablespoons Kirsch

Preparation time: 25 minutes, plus freezing
Cooking time: 25 minutes

Use the milk, vanilla pod or vanilla essence, egg yolks and caster sugar to make a vanilla custard (see Basic Vanilla Ice Cream, page 8). Allow to cool, then pour the custard into a freezer container and freeze for about 1½ hours until mushy.
Beat the cream until it forms soft peaks. Fold the cream, almonds and Kirsch into the frozen custard, and freeze. Beat the mixture three times, at hourly intervals. Cover, seal and freeze.
Serves 4–6

Walnut ice cream

Metric	Imperial
450 ml milk	¾ pint milk
1 vanilla pod	1 vanilla pod
4 egg yolks	4 egg yolks
100 g soft brown sugar	4 oz soft brown sugar
150 ml double or whipping cream	5 fl oz double or whipping cream
100 g walnut halves, finely chopped	4 oz walnut halves, finely chopped

Preparation time: 25 minutes, plus freezing
Cooking time: 25 minutes

Use the milk, vanilla pod, egg yolks and soft brown sugar to make a vanilla custard (see Basic Vanilla Ice Cream, page 8). Pour into a large mixing bowl and allow to go cold.
Beat the cream until it forms soft peaks and fold into the custard with the walnuts. Pour into a freezer container and freeze. Beat the mixture twice, at hourly intervals. Cover, seal and freeze.
Serves 4–6

Apricot and almond ice cream

Metric	Imperial
225 g dried apricots, soaked overnight in 150 ml water	8 oz dried apricots, soaked overnight in ¼ pint water
2 strips lemon peel	2 strips lemon peel
450 ml single cream	15 fl oz single cream
1 vanilla pod	1 vanilla pod
3 egg yolks	3 egg yolks
100 g caster sugar	4 oz caster sugar
50 g ground almonds	2 oz ground almonds
3 drops almond essence	3 drops almond essence
150 ml double or whipping cream	5 fl oz double or whipping cream

Preparation time: 20 minutes, plus overnight soaking and freezing
Cooking time: 35 minutes

Because of the ground almonds this delicious ice cream is slightly drier in texture.

Put the apricots, the soaking liquid and lemon peel in a saucepan. Simmer over a gentle heat until the apricots are soft. Discard the lemon peel and allow to cool slightly.
Liquidize the apricots to a purée with their cooking juice. Allow to go cold.
Use the single cream, vanilla pod, egg yolks and caster sugar to make a vanilla custard (see Basic Vanilla Ice Cream, page 8). Pour into a large mixing bowl and allow to go cold.
Stir the apricot purée, ground almonds and almond essence into the custard. Beat the double or whipping cream until it forms soft peaks and fold into the mixture. Pour into a freezer container and freeze. Beat the mixture twice, at hourly intervals. Cover, seal and freeze.
Serves 4–6

Clockwise from left: Almond and Kirsch ice cream with orange sauce; Walnut ice cream; Apricot and almond ice cream

SYRUPS AND SAUCES

Syrups and sauces are delicious with any of the custard-based and cream-based ice creams. You can choose any sauce or syrup to use with the various ice creams, but serving suggestions are given with each recipe in this chapter. Syrups may also be used for Knickerbocker Glories (see pages 70, 71).

Most of the sauces can be stored in the refrigerator in sealed plastic containers. The syrups can be kept in sterilized bottles or jars, which should be sealed with corks, screw-topped lids, or waxed discs and cellophane.

Because of their high sugar content it is best to prepare syrups in enamel pans. Wooden spoons and nylon sieves are best used throughout this section.

Sterilizing bottles and jars
Wash the bottles or jars, and their corks or screw-topped lids thoroughly, rinse them in hot water and drain. About half an hour before using, put the clean bottles, jars, corks or screw-topped lids into a preheated oven at 140°C, 275°F, Gas Mark 1 to sterilize and warm them and prevent cracking when filling them with hot syrup.

Black cherry syrup

Metric
300 ml black cherry juice
2 × 15 ml spoons cherry
   brandy
100 g granulated sugar

Imperial
½ pint black cherry juice
2 tablespoons cherry
   brandy
4 oz granulated sugar

Preparation time: 15 minutes
Cooking time: about 10 minutes

Pour the cherry juice and the cherry brandy into an enamel saucepan and add the sugar. Heat gently until the sugar has dissolved. Increase the heat and cook rapidly until the smooth stage is reached (see page 6). Remove any scum which forms during the sugar boiling time.
Cool slightly, then strain the syrup into a warm, sterilized bottle. Allow to go cold, then seal. The syrup will store in a cool place for 2–3 weeks.
Serve with Black Cherry (page 13), Vanilla (page 8), or Apricot and Almond Ice Cream (page 16).
Makes 250 ml/8 fl oz

From left: Black cherry syrup with apricot and almond ice cream; Strawberry syrup with vanilla ice cream; Melba sauce with vanilla ice cream

Strawberry syrup

Metric
1 kg fresh strawberries,
   hulled and roughly
   chopped
1 kg granulated sugar
1 × 15 ml spoon lemon
   juice

Imperial
2 lb fresh strawberries,
   hulled and roughly
   chopped
2 lb granulated sugar
1 tablespoon lemon
   juice

Preparation time: 15 minutes, plus overnight soaking, and draining
Cooking time: about 5 minutes

If you do not have a jelly bag a fine nylon sieve can be substituted, although the result will be a cloudier syrup.

Put the chopped strawberries in a large bowl. Pour the sugar over the fruit and cover with a clean cloth. Leave to stand overnight to let the sugar draw the juice from the fruit.
Pour the fruit and sugar into a jelly bag and allow the juice to drip into an enamel saucepan. Add the lemon juice and heat gently until the sugar has dissolved. Increase the heat and cook rapidly until the smooth stage is reached (see page 6). Remove any scum which forms during the cooking time.
Cool slightly, then pour the syrup into a warm, sterilized bottle. Allow to go cold, then seal. The syrup will store in a cool place for at least 1 month.
Serve with Vanilla (page 8) or Strawberry Ice Cream (page 27), or Cassata (page 9).
Makes about 350 ml/12 fl oz

Melba sauce

Metric
450 g fresh raspberries,
   hulled
100 g icing sugar, sifted
2 × 5 ml spoons lemon
   juice

Imperial
1 lb fresh raspberries,
   hulled
4 oz icing sugar, sifted
2 teaspoons lemon
   juice

Preparation time: 20 minutes

Liquidize the raspberries, or if preferred rub them through a nylon sieve using a wooden spoon, to remove the pips. Stir the icing sugar gently into the purée, and add the lemon juice. The sauce will store for up to 2 weeks in a sealed container in the refrigerator, or in a freezer for up to 3 months.
Serve with Vanilla (page 8) or Raspberry Ice Cream (page 27), or pour over Old-fashioned Peach Melba (page 63) or Muesli Banana Splits (page 66).
Makes 300 ml/½ pint

Butterscotch sauce

Metric	Imperial
50 g butter	2 oz butter
50 g demerara sugar	2 oz demerara sugar
50 g golden syrup	2 oz golden syrup
150 ml milk	¼ pint milk

Preparation time: 10 minutes
Cooking time: about 10 minutes

Put the butter, sugar and golden syrup in a heavy-based saucepan. Heat gently until the sugar has dissolved. Increase the heat and cook rapidly until the soft ball stage is reached (see page 6).
Cool slightly, then slowly beat in the milk. Allow to go cold, pour into a sterilized bottle or plastic container and seal. The sauce will store in a cool place for 2–3 weeks.
Serve with Ginger (page 15), Rum and Raisin (page 11), or Vanilla Ice Cream (page 8).
Makes 300 ml/½ pint

Hot chocolate fudge sauce

Metric	Imperial
50 g plain chocolate, broken into small pieces	2 oz plain chocolate, broken into small pieces
2 × 15 ml spoons golden syrup	2 tablespoons golden syrup
100 g caster sugar	4 oz caster sugar
1 × 15 ml spoon cocoa	1 tablespoon cocoa
5 × 15 ml spoons hot water	5 tablespoons hot water
25 g butter	1 oz butter
1 × 15 ml spoon cold water	1 tablespoon cold water

Preparation time: 5 minutes
Cooking time: about 10 minutes

Put the chocolate in a heavy-based saucepan with the golden syrup, sugar, cocoa and hot water. Stir over a gentle heat until melted. Increase the heat and cook rapidly, without stirring, until the soft ball stage is reached (see page 6). Remove from the heat and gently stir in the butter and cold water.
Serve immediately with Vanilla (page 8), Walnut (page 16), or Pear Ice Cream (page 36).
Makes 175 ml/6 fl oz

From left: Vanilla ice cream with sauces: Butterscotch sauce; Hot chocolate fudge sauce; Apricot sauce; Hot chocolate sauce

Apricot sauce

Metric
225 g fresh apricots,
   halved and stoned
150 ml water
50 g demerara sugar
1 × 5 ml spoon lemon juice
1 × 5 ml spoon arrowroot
1 × 15 ml spoon water

Imperial
8 oz fresh apricots,
   halved and stoned
¼ pint water
2 oz demerara sugar
1 teaspoon lemon juice
1 teaspoon arrowroot
1 tablespoon water

Preparation time: 25 minutes
Cooking time: 15 minutes

Put the apricots into a saucepan with the water and simmer over a gentle heat until the fruit is very soft. Allow to cool.
Meanwhile, crack the apricot stones, remove and finely chop the kernels. Using a wooden spoon rub the apricots through a nylon sieve into a saucepan. Add the kernels to the purée with the sugar and lemon juice. Return the mixture to the heat. Blend the arrowroot with the water and use to thicken the sauce. This sauce will keep in a sealed container in a refrigerator for up to 1 week.
Serve hot or cold with Vanilla (page 8), Ratafia (page 28), or Pear Ice Cream (page 36).
Makes about 350 ml/12 fl oz

Hot chocolate sauce

Metric
225 g plain chocolate,
   broken into small pieces
100 g caster sugar
300 ml hot water
pinch of salt
25 g butter, cut into small
   pieces

Imperial
8 oz plain chocolate,
   broken into small pieces
4 oz caster sugar
½ pint hot water
pinch of salt
1 oz butter, cut into small
   pieces

Preparation time: 10 minutes
Cooking time: 10 minutes

Put the chocolate in a heavy-based saucepan with the sugar, hot water and salt. Stir over a gentle heat until melted. Increase the heat and cook rapidly until the mixture becomes syrupy. It should just coat the back of a wooden spoon.
Cool slightly, then beat in the butter. The sauce can be made a few hours in advance and reheated. Before serving, gently reheat in a double saucepan, stirring gently as the mixture melts.
Serve hot with Chocolate and Orange (page 10), Vanilla (page 8), or Oatcake Ice Cream (page 14).
Makes about 300 ml/½ pint

Hot rum sauce

Metric
75 g butter, creamed
225 g caster sugar
2 eggs, separated
1 × 15 ml spoon rum

Imperial
3 oz butter, creamed
8 oz caster sugar
2 eggs, separated
1 tablespoon rum

Preparation time: 10 minutes
Cooking time: 20 minutes

This sauce can be partly prepared a few hours in advance, then reheated gently in a double saucepan, and the egg whites and rum added before serving.

Put the creamed butter and the sugar in a double saucepan. Beat the egg yolks thoroughly and add them to the pan. Place over a gentle heat and stir the mixture until it thickens, keeping the water in the base of the double boiler at simmering point to ensure the mixture does not curdle.
When the sauce has thickened enough to coat the back of a wooden spoon, beat the egg whites until stiff and fold them into the sauce with the rum.
Serve immediately with Rum and Raisin (page 11), Vanilla (page 8), or Grape Ice Cream (page 37).
Makes 350 ml/12 fl oz

Hot rum sauce with grape ice cream; Hot caramel sauce with honey and lemon ice cream; Hot coffee sauce with vanilla ice cream

Hot caramel sauce

Metric
350 ml water
75 g caster sugar
juice of ½ lemon

Imperial
12 fl oz water
3 oz caster sugar
juice of ½ lemon

Preparation time: 10 minutes
Cooking time: 20 minutes

Pour 150 ml/5 fl oz of the water into a heavy-based saucepan and add the sugar. Heat gently until the sugar has dissolved. Increase the heat and cook rapidly until the syrup begins to caramelize and is golden brown. The temperature will be 175°C, 350°F on a sugar thermometer.
Remove from the heat and gradually stir in the remaining water with the lemon juice. Gently reheat the sauce before serving. This sauce will keep in a sealed container in a refrigerator for 3–4 weeks.
Serve hot with Vanilla (page 8), Walnut (page 16), or Honey and Lemon Ice Cream (page 12).
Makes 300 ml/½ pint

Hot coffee sauce

Metric	*Imperial*
300 ml strong black coffee	*½ pint strong black coffee*
175 g caster sugar	*6 oz caster sugar*
1 × 15 ml spoon cornflour	*1 tablespoon cornflour*
2 × 15 ml spoons water	*2 tablespoons water*
2 × 15 ml spoons coffee	*2 tablespoons coffee*
liqueur	*liqueur*

Preparation time: 10 minutes
Cooking time: 10 minutes

Put the coffee and sugar in a heavy-based saucepan and bring slowly to the boil. Simmer for 5 minutes. Blend the cornflour with the water and use to thicken the coffee mixture. Stir in the coffee liqueur. Serve immediately with Mocha (page 11), Vanilla (page 8), or Earl Grey Ice Cream (page 15). Makes about 300 ml/½ pint

Prune syrup

Metric	Imperial
20 prunes, soaked overnight in 600 ml cold tea	20 prunes, soaked overnight in 1 pint cold tea
225 g granulated sugar	8 oz granulated sugar
juice of ½ lemon	juice of ½ lemon

Preparation time: 10 minutes, plus overnight soaking
Cooking time: 35–40 minutes

Put the prunes with the soaking liquid in a saucepan and simmer gently for about 25–30 minutes until tender. Strain the liquid into a heavy-based saucepan and add the sugar and lemon juice. Heat gently until the sugar has dissolved. Increase the heat and cook rapidly until the smooth stage is reached (see page 6). Remove any scum which forms during the sugar boiling time.
Cool slightly, then pour the syrup into a warm steril-ized bottle. Allow to go cold, then seal. The syrup will store in a cool place for at least 1 month.
Serve with Vanilla (page 8) or Oatcake Ice Cream (page 14), or with Plum and Gin Sorbet (page 43).
Makes about 350 ml/12 fl oz

Hot lemon and orange sauce

Metric	Imperial
15 g cornflour	½ oz cornflour
300 ml milk	½ pint milk
grated rind and juice of 1 lemon	grated rind and juice of 1 lemon
grated rind and juice of 1 orange	grated rind and juice of 1 orange
3 × 15 ml spoons golden syrup	3 tablespoons golden syrup

Preparation time: 10 minutes
Cooking time: 10 minutes

Blend the cornflour with 3 × 15 ml spoons/3 table-spoons of the milk. Pour the remaining milk into a saucepan and heat gently. Add the grated fruit rinds and bring to the boil.
Pour the hot milk slowly on to the cornflour, stirring constantly. Return the sauce to the pan and simmer for 3 minutes, stirring gently. Stir in the fruit juices and the golden syrup.
Serve immediately with Gooseberry (page 37), Vanilla (page 8), or Chocolate and Orange Ice Cream (page 10).
Makes 350 ml/12 fl oz

Orange syrup

Metric	Imperial
6 oranges	6 oranges
water	water
750 g granulated sugar	1½ lb granulated sugar

Preparation time: 15 minutes
Cooking time: about 10 minutes

Grate the rind from 2 of the oranges and set aside. Squeeze the juice from all the oranges, strain and make up to 600 ml/1 pint with water.
Pour the orange juice into an enamel saucepan and add the sugar. Heat gently until the sugar has dissolved. Increase the heat and cook rapidly until the smooth stage is reached (see page 6). Remove any scum that forms during the cooking time.
Put the grated orange rind into a fine nylon sieve and strain the syrup through it. Cool slightly, then pour into warm, sterilized bottles. Allow to go cold, then seal. The syrup will store in a cool place for up to 1 month.
Serve with Lychee (page 30) or Grape Ice Cream (page 37), or Citrus Sorbet (page 39).
Makes about 600 ml/1 pint

Redcurrant syrup

Metric	Imperial
1 kg redcurrants, topped and tailed	2 lb redcurrants, topped and tailed
about 450 g granulated sugar	about 1 lb granulated sugar

Preparation time: 25 minutes
Cooking time: 5–6 minutes

Liquidize the redcurrants to a purée. Rub the purée through a fine nylon sieve using a wooden spoon. Measure the juice and pour it into an enamel saucepan. To each 150 ml/¼ pint of redcurrant juice add 225 g/8 oz granulated sugar.
Heat gently until the sugar has dissolved. Increase the heat and simmer rapidly until the smooth stage is reached (see page 6). Remove any scum which forms during the cooking time.
Cool slightly, then pour the syrup into a warm, sterilized bottle. The syrup will store in a cool place for up to 2 weeks.
Serve with Vanilla (page 8), Pear (page 36), or Sparkling Wine Ice Cream (page 32).
Makes about 300 ml/½ pint

Clockwise: Orange syrup; Redcurrant syrup; Hot lemon and orange sauce with chocolate and orange ice cream; Prune syrup

CREAM-BASED ICE CREAM

Cream-based ice creams are often more colourful and can have more flavour than custard-based ice creams. Because the ingredients can be expensive evaporated milk makes an excellent alternative for a cheaper ice cream which is also especially popular with children.

Unless you are using an ice-cream maker, it is best to freeze the basic mixture to a mushy, partly frozen, consistency before adding the cream. In most of these recipes the ice cream is beaten a number of times at hourly intervals during the final freezing process (see page 4). This incorporates the flavouring with the cream and ensures that no ice crystals form to spoil the texture. In general the higher the ratio of cream to basic flavouring the less beating is necessary.

As with custard-based ices, the total freezing time should be at least 3–4 hours and the ice creams are best removed from the freezer to the refrigerator 45 minutes before serving.

From left: Raspberry ice cream with walnut tiles; Strawberry ice cream with strawberry syrup; Blackberry and apple ice cream with sponge fingers

Strawberry ice cream

Metric
1 kg fresh or frozen
   strawberries, hulled
1 × 15 ml spoon lemon
   juice
450 g icing sugar, sifted
600 ml double or whipping
   cream

Imperial
2 lb fresh or frozen
   strawberries, hulled
1 tablespoon lemon
   juice
1 lb icing sugar, sifted
20 fl oz double or whipping
   cream

Preparation time: 30 minutes, plus freezing

Liquidize the strawberries to a purée. Alternatively, rub through a nylon sieve using a wooden spoon. Stir in the lemon juice. Gradually add the icing sugar, stirring well between each addition.
Beat the cream until it forms soft peaks and fold into the strawberry mixture. Pour into a freezer container and freeze. Beat once after 1 hour, then cover, seal and freeze.
Serves 6–8

Variations:
Use blackcurrants, raspberries, blackberries or loganberries instead of strawberries.

Raspberry ice cream

Metric
1 × 400 g can evaporated
   milk, chilled overnight
450 g fresh or frozen
   raspberries
100 g icing sugar, sifted

Imperial
1 × 14 oz can evaporated
   milk, chilled overnight
1 lb fresh or frozen
   raspberries
4 oz icing sugar, sifted

Preparation time: 20 minutes, plus overnight chilling, and freezing

Beat the chilled evaporated milk until it becomes thick and frothy.
Liquidize the raspberries to a purée, or if preferred rub them through a nylon sieve using a wooden spoon to remove the pips. Beat the icing sugar into the evaporated milk and stir in the raspberry purée.
Pour into a freezer container and freeze. Beat the mixture twice, at hourly intervals. Cover, seal and freeze.
Serves 4–6

Blackberry and apple ice cream

Metric
225 g frozen or fresh
   blackberries
2 cooking apples, peeled
   and sliced
2 × 15 ml spoons Calvados
   or 1 × 15 ml spoon
   brandy
300 ml double or whipping
   cream
50 g caster sugar

Imperial
8 oz frozen or fresh
   blackberries
2 cooking apples, peeled
   and sliced
2 tablespoons Calvados
   or 1 tablespoon
   brandy
10 fl oz double or whipping
   cream
2 oz caster sugar

Preparation time: 15 minutes, plus freezing
Cooking time: 15 minutes

Simmer the blackberries and apples together over a low heat, adding a little water if necessary to prevent the fruit from burning. When fully softened, remove from the heat and allow to go cold. Stir in the Calvados or brandy.
Beat the cream until it forms soft peaks and fold in the sugar. Fold the fruit into the cream and sugar. Pour into a freezer container and freeze. Beat the mixture twice, at hourly intervals. Cover, seal and freeze.

Serves 4–6

Butterscotch ice cream

Metric	Imperial
100 g dark soft brown sugar	4 oz dark soft brown sugar
150 ml water	¼ pint water
25 g butter	1 oz butter
2 × 5 ml spoons lemon juice	2 teaspoons lemon juice
2 × 5 ml spoons arrowroot, blended with a little water	2 teaspoons arrowroot, blended with a little water
1 × 400 g can evaporated milk, chilled overnight	1 × 14 oz can evaporated milk, chilled overnight
3 drops vanilla essence	3 drops vanilla essence

Preparation time: 15 minutes, plus overnight chilling, and freezing
Cooking time: 15 minutes

Make a butterscotch sauce by putting the sugar and water in a saucepan and heating gently until the sugar has dissolved. Add the butter and lemon juice and cook rapidly for 5 minutes, without stirring.
Stir in the arrowroot, and allow the sauce to thicken over a gentle heat. Set aside to cool.
Beat the chilled evaporated milk until thick and frothy. Fold in the cooled butterscotch sauce with the vanilla essence.
Pour into a freezer container and freeze. Beat the mixture twice, at hourly intervals. Cover, seal and freeze.
Serves 6

Chocolate flake and brandy ice cream

Metric	Imperial
1 × 400 g can evaporated milk, chilled overnight	1 × 14 oz can evaporated milk, chilled overnight
100 g icing sugar, sifted	4 oz icing sugar, sifted
2 large bars chocolate flake, crumbled	2 large bars chocolate flake, crumbled
1 × 15 ml spoon brandy	1 tablespoon brandy

Preparation time: 15 minutes, plus overnight chilling, and freezing

Beat the chilled evaporated milk until thick and frothy. Gradually beat in the icing sugar, then stir in the chocolate flake and the brandy.
Pour into a freezer container and freeze. Beat the mixture twice, at hourly intervals. Cover, seal and freeze.
Serves 4–6

Caramel ice cream

Metric	Imperial
75 g caster sugar	3 oz caster sugar
1 × 15 ml spoon water	1 tablespoon water
600 ml single cream	20 fl oz single cream
4 egg yolks, beaten	4 egg yolks, beaten
150 ml double or whipping cream	5 fl oz double or whipping cream

Preparation time: 15 minutes, plus freezing
Cooking time: 20 minutes

Put the sugar and the water into a heavy-based saucepan and heat very gently until dissolved. Increase the heat and boil steadily, without stirring, until the sugar begins to caramelize and is golden brown. The temperature on a sugar thermometer will be 175 °C, 350 °F.
Heat the single cream in a saucepan to boiling point and beat the hot caramel into it. Allow the mixture to go cold. Stir in the beaten egg yolks. Pour into a freezer container and freeze for about 1½ hours until mushy.
Beat the cream until it forms soft peaks. Fold into the frozen caramel mixture and freeze. Beat the mixture twice, at hourly intervals. Cover, seal and freeze.
Serves 4–6

Ratafia ice cream

Metric	Imperial
100 g ratafia biscuits, crushed	4 oz ratafia biscuits, crushed
150 ml sherry	¼ pint sherry
300 ml double or whipping cream	10 fl oz double or whipping cream
300 ml single cream	10 fl oz single cream
50 g icing sugar, sifted	2 oz icing sugar, sifted
25 g chopped nuts	1 oz chopped nuts

Preparation time: 15 minutes, plus soaking, and freezing

Put the crushed ratafia biscuits into a small bowl and cover with the sherry. Leave for about 20 minutes to allow the sherry to soak into the biscuits.
Beat the two creams together, then beat in the icing sugar. Fold in the soaked ratafia biscuits and the chopped nuts. Put into a freezer container and freeze. Beat the mixture twice, at hourly intervals. Cover, seal and freeze.
Serves 4–6

From left: Chocolate flake ice cream; Ratafia ice cream with hot caramel sauce; Butterscotch ice cream; Caramel ice cream

Lychee ice cream

Metric	Imperial
1 × 400 can evaporated milk, chilled overnight	1 × 14 oz can evaporated milk, chilled overnight
100 g icing sugar, sifted	4 oz icing sugar, sifted
1 × 500 g can lychees, drained and chopped	1 × 1¼ lb can lychees, drained and chopped

Preparation time: 15 minutes, plus overnight chilling, and freezing

The subtle flavour of the lychees delicately flavours the evaporated milk in this recipe.

Beat the chilled evaporated milk until thick and frothy. Beat the icing sugar into the evaporated milk, then fold in the chopped lychees.
Pour into a freezer container and freeze. Beat the mixture three times, at hourly intervals to prevent the fruit from sinking. Cover, seal and freeze.
Serves 4–6

Banana ice cream

Metric	Imperial
450 g ripe bananas	1 lb ripe bananas
1 × 15 ml spoon lemon juice	1 tablespoon lemon juice
2 × 15 ml spoons white rum (optional)	2 tablespoons white rum (optional)
50 g soft brown sugar	2 oz soft brown sugar
300 ml double or whipping cream	10 fl oz double or whipping cream

Preparation time: 15 minutes, plus freezing

Peel the bananas and mash them with the lemon juice, rum and the sugar until smooth. Alternatively, use a liquidizer. Beat the cream until it forms soft peaks and gently fold into the banana mixture.
Put the mixture into a freezer container and freeze for about 1½ hours until mushy.
Gently beat the mixture and continue freezing for a further hour. Beat again, then cover, seal and freeze.
Serves 4–6

Lychee ice cream; Banana ice cream; Mango ice cream; Passion fruit ice cream

Mango ice cream

Metric	Imperial
300 ml water	½ pint water
100 g caster sugar	4 oz caster sugar
1 ripe mango, peeled, halved and stoned	1 ripe mango, peeled, halved and stoned
2 × 15 ml spoons lemon juice	2 tablespoons lemon juice
150 ml double or whipping cream	5 fl oz double or whipping cream

Preparation time: 20 minutes, plus freezing
Cooking time: about 8 minutes

Put the water and sugar into a heavy-based saucepan and heat gently until the sugar has dissolved. Increase the heat and cook rapidly until the thread stage is reached (see page 6). Remove from the heat and cool.
Liquidize or sieve the mango flesh with the lemon juice to a purée. Stir the purée into the syrup. Put the mixture into a freezer container and freeze for about 1½ hours until mushy.
Beat the cream until it forms soft peaks. Fold into the frozen mango mixture and freeze. Beat the mixture twice, at hourly intervals. Cover, seal and freeze.
Serves 4–6

Passion fruit ice cream

Metric	Imperial
8 ripe passion fruits	8 ripe passion fruits
water	water
100 g caster sugar	4 oz caster sugar
1 × 5 ml spoon lemon juice	1 teaspoon lemon juice
300 ml double or whipping cream	10 fl oz double or whipping cream

Preparation time: 20 minutes, plus freezing
Cooking time: about 8 minutes

Cut the passion fruits in half and scoop out the pips and flesh. Strain the juice and discard any pips. Make the juice up to 300 ml/½ pint with water.
Pour the liquid into a heavy-based saucepan, stir in the caster sugar and heat gently until the sugar has dissolved. Increase the heat and cook rapidly until the thread stage is reached (see page 6). Remove from the heat and stir in the lemon juice.
Pour into a freezer container and freeze for about 1½ hours until mushy.
Beat the cream until it forms soft peaks. Fold into the frozen syrup mixture. Cover, seal and freeze.
Serve with Melba Sauce (page 19).
Serves 4–6

Cranberry ice cream

Metric	Imperial
250 ml water	8 fl oz water
350 g fresh cranberries	12 oz fresh cranberries
3 × 15 ml spoons orange juice	3 tablespoons orange juice
100 g caster sugar	4 oz caster sugar
2 × 15 ml spoons port	2 tablespoons port
150 ml double or whipping cream	5 fl oz double or whipping cream
pinch of bicarbonate of soda	pinch of bicarbonate of soda

Preparation time: 20 minutes, plus freezing
Cooking time: about 25 minutes

Put the water and cranberries into a saucepan and simmer gently until soft. Strain the juice and make up to 300 ml/½ pint with the orange juice, adding more water if necessary.
Pour the liquid into a saucepan, add the sugar and heat gently until the sugar has dissolved. Increase the heat and cook rapidly until the thread stage is reached (see page 6). Remove from the heat and cool. Liquidize the cranberries to a purée, then rub through a nylon sieve using a wooden spoon to remove the skins. Fold the purée and the port into the syrup. Pour into a freezer container and freeze for about 1½ hours until mushy.
Beat the cream until it forms soft peaks. Fold into the frozen cranberry mixture and freeze. Beat the mixture twice, at hourly intervals. Cover, seal and freeze.
Serves 4–6

Sparkling wine ice cream

Metric	Imperial
350 g caster sugar	12 oz caster sugar
300 ml water	½ pint water
3 × 15 ml spoons orange juice	3 tablespoons orange juice
1 × 15 ml spoon brandy	1 tablespoon brandy
450 ml sparkling white wine	¾ pint sparkling white wine
150 ml double or whipping cream	5 fl oz double or whipping cream

Preparation time: 15 minutes, plus freezing
Cooking time: about 8 minutes

Put the water and sugar into a heavy-based saucepan and gently heat until the sugar has dissolved. Increase the heat and cook rapidly until the thread stage is reached (see page 6). Remove from the heat and cool. Mix the orange juice, brandy and sparkling wine together and add to the syrup. Pour the mixture into a freezer container and freeze for about 1½ hours until mushy.
Beat the cream until it forms soft peaks. Fold into the frozen mixture and freeze. Beat the mixture three times, at hourly intervals. Cover, seal and freeze.
Serves 4–6

From left: Cranberry ice cream; Sparkling wine ice cream;
Sweet peppermint ice cream; Blackcurrant ice cream

Sweet peppermint ice cream

Metric
175 g caster sugar
450 ml water
6 drops peppermint essence
450 ml double or whipping cream
1¼ × 15 ml spoons finely chopped fresh mint
1½ × 5 ml spoons white Crème de Menthe

Imperial
6 oz caster sugar
¾ pint water
6 drops peppermint essence
15 fl oz double or whipping cream
1½ tablespoons finely chopped fresh mint
1½ teaspoons white Crème de Menthe

Preparation time: 15 minutes
Cooking time: about 8 minutes

Put the water and sugar into a heavy-based saucepan and heat gently until the sugar has dissolved. Increase the heat and cook rapidly until the thread stage is reached (see page 6). Remove from the heat, stir in the peppermint essence and cool.
Pour the syrup into a freezer container and freeze for about 1½ hours until mushy.
Beat the cream until it forms soft peaks. Fold the cream, chopped mint and Crème de Menthe into the frozen syrup. Cover, seal and freeze.
Serves 4–6

Blackcurrant ice cream

Metric
450 g fresh or frozen blackcurrants, topped and tailed
175 g caster sugar
300 ml water
1 × 5 ml spoon lemon juice
2 drops cochineal
350 ml double or whipping cream

Imperial
1 lb fresh or frozen blackcurrants, topped and tailed
6 oz caster sugar
½ pint water
1 teaspoon lemon juice
2 drops cochineal
12 fl oz double or whipping cream

Preparation time: 15 minutes, plus freezing
Cooking time: 6–8 minutes

Put the blackcurrants in a saucepan with the sugar, water, lemon juice and cochineal. Simmer over a gentle heat for 6–8 minutes until the blackcurrants are soft and the juice is syrupy. Allow to cool, then liquidize to a purée. Alternatively, rub through a nylon sieve using a wooden spoon so that the skins are removed.
Beat the cream until it forms soft peaks. Fold into the blackcurrant purée, pour into a freezer container and freeze. Beat the mixture twice, at hourly intervals. Cover, seal and freeze.
Serves 6

Lemon and soft cheese ice cream

Metric
1 × 400 g can evaporated
  milk, chilled overnight
75 g icing sugar
100 g full fat soft cheese,
  beaten until soft
grated rind and juice of
  2 lemons

Imperial
1 × 14 oz can evaporated
  milk, chilled overnight
3 oz icing sugar
4 oz full fat soft cheese,
  beaten until soft
grated rind and juice of
  2 lemons

Preparation time: 15 minutes, plus overnight chilling, and freezing

Beat the chilled evaporated milk until thick and frothy. Beat the sugar into the evaporated milk. Fold the softened cheese into the evaporated milk mixture, then add the lemon rind and juice.
Pour into a freezer container and freeze. Beat the mixture twice, at hourly intervals. Cover, seal and freeze.
Serves 4–6

Camembert ice cream

Metric
225 g soft ripe Camembert
 (1 whole cheese),
 broken into small pieces
100 g cottage cheese
250 ml double or whipping
 cream
few drops of Tabasco
 sauce
freshly ground black
 pepper
fingers of toast, to serve

Imperial
8 oz soft ripe Camembert
 (1 whole cheese),
 broken into small pieces
4 oz cottage cheese
8 fl oz double or whipping
 cream
few drops of Tabasco
 sauce
freshly ground black
 pepper
fingers of toast, to serve

Preparation time: 20 minutes, plus freezing

Serve this ice cream as an interesting and unusual starter.

Put the cottage cheese and cream in a large bowl and beat together until nearly smooth. Beat the Camembert into the cream and cottage cheese mixture. Add a little Tabasco sauce, and pepper to taste. Put into a freezer container, cover, seal and freeze.
Serve as a starter with fingers of toast.
Serves 4–6

From left: Lemon and soft cheese ice cream; Camembert ice cream; Goat cheese and hazelnut ice cream

Goat cheese and hazelnut ice cream

Metric
225 g goat cheese
150 ml single cream
150 ml double or whipping
 cream
1 × 5 ml spoon lemon juice
freshly ground black
 pepper
50 g hazelnuts

Imperial
8 oz goat cheese
5 fl oz single cream
5 fl oz double or whipping
 cream
1 teaspoon lemon juice
freshly ground black
 pepper
2 oz hazelnuts

To serve:
watercress or chopped
 parsley
fingers of toast

To serve:
watercress or chopped
 parsley
fingers of toast

Preparation time: 20 minutes, plus freezing
Cooking time: 5 minutes

This makes an original and delicious starter, but because this ice cream has a firmer texture than others it needs to be defrosted for 1½ hours at room temperature before serving.

Put the goat cheese, the two creams and lemon juice into a large mixing bowl. Beat together, adding pepper to taste.
Toast the hazelnuts under a preheated low grill, so that the skins are easier to remove, turning them with a fork to ensure even browning. Remove the skins, then chop the nuts roughly and fold into the cheese mixture. Put the mixture into a freezer container, cover, seal and freeze.
Garnish with watercress or parsley and serve as a starter with fingers of toast.
Serves 4–6

Pear ice cream

Preparation time: 20 minutes, plus freezing
Cooking time: 25 minutes

Metric
450 g ripe pears, peeled,
    cored and chopped
50 g butter
25 g caster sugar
4 × 15 ml spoons water
1 × 15 ml spoon orange
    juice
strip of lemon peel
2 egg yolks, beaten
300 ml double or whipping
    cream

Imperial
1 lb ripe pears, peeled,
    cored and chopped
2 oz butter
1 oz caster sugar
4 tablespoons water
1 tablespoon orange
    juice
strip of lemon peel
2 egg yolks, beaten
10 fl oz double or whipping
    cream

Put the pears into a pan with the butter, sugar, water, orange juice, and lemon peel. Simmer gently, uncovered, until the pears are very soft and the liquid is reduced by half.

Liquidize the mixture to a purée. Alternatively rub through a nylon sieve using a wooden spoon. Return the purée to the pan with the beaten egg yolks. Heat gently, stirring all the time, until the mixture has thickened. Do not allow to boil. Remove from the heat and allow to go cold.

Beat the cream until it forms soft peaks and fold gently into the pear mixture. Pour into a freezer container, cover, seal and freeze.

Serves 4–6

Melon and ginger ice cream

Metric	Imperial
750 g ripe honeydew melon	1½ lb ripe honeydew melon
water	water
100 g caster sugar	4 oz caster sugar
2 × 15 ml spoons lemon juice	2 tablespoons lemon juice
250 ml double or whipping cream	8 fl oz double or whipping cream
25 g piece stem ginger, thinly sliced	1 oz piece stem ginger, thinly sliced
1 × 15 ml spoon ginger syrup	1 tablespoon ginger syrup

Preparation time: 20 minutes, plus freezing
Cooking time: about 8 minutes

If preferred, the stem ginger and syrup can be left out of the recipe. Other types of melon can be used, each will give the ice cream its own deliciously subtle flavour.

Cut the melon in half and scoop out the the pips. Remove the melon flesh and liquidize or sieve to a purée. Strain any juice through a nylon sieve and make up to 300 ml/½ pint with water.
Pour the liquid into a heavy-based saucepan, add the sugar and heat gently until the sugar has dissolved. Increase the heat and cook rapidly until the thread stage is reached (see page 6). Remove from the heat and cool.
Add the melon purée and lemon juice to the syrup. Put the mixture into a freezer container and freeze for about 1½ hours until mushy.
Beat the cream until it forms soft peaks. Fold into the frozen melon mixture, with the sliced ginger and the ginger syrup, and freeze. Beat the mixture twice, at hourly intervals. Cover, seal and freeze.
Serves 4–6

Clockwise from top: Pear ice cream; Gooseberry ice cream with langues de chat; Grape ice cream; Melon and ginger ice cream

Grape ice cream

Metric	Imperial
450 g black grapes, stalks removed	1 lb black grapes, stalks removed
100 g caster sugar	4 oz caster sugar
150 ml double or whipping cream	5 fl oz double or whipping cream
2 egg whites	2 egg whites

Preparation time: 25 minutes, plus freezing

Liquidize the grapes to a purée, then rub through a nylon sieve using a wooden spoon, to remove the skin and pips. Beat in the sugar. Put the mixture into a freezer container and freeze for about 1½ hours until mushy.
Beat the cream until it forms soft peaks and fold gently into the frozen grape mixture. Beat the egg whites until they form soft peaks. Fold into the mixture and freeze. Beat the mixture twice, at hourly intervals. Cover, seal and freeze.
Serves 4–6

Gooseberry ice cream

Metric	Imperial
150 ml water	¼ pint water
450 g gooseberries, topped and tailed	1 lb gooseberries, topped and tailed
50 g caster sugar	2 oz caster sugar
1 × 15 ml spoon finely grated orange rind	1 tablespoon finely grated orange rind
2 egg yolks, beaten	2 egg yolks, beaten
150 ml double or whipping cream	5 fl oz double or whipping cream
2 egg whites	2 egg whites

Preparation time: 20 minutes, plus freezing
Cooking time: 15 minutes

Put the water in a saucepan with the gooseberries, sugar and orange rind. Simmer over a gentle heat until the gooseberries are very soft. Allow to cool, then liquidize to a purée. Alternatively rub through a nylon sieve using a wooden spoon.
Stir the egg yolks into the gooseberry purée. Put the mixture into a freezer container and freeze for about 1½ hours until mushy.
Beat the cream until it forms soft peaks and fold gently into the frozen gooseberry mixture. Beat the egg whites until stiff and fold them in.
Return the mixture to the freezer and beat after 1 hour. Cover, seal and freeze.
Serves 4–6

SORBETS

Sorbets are much lighter, fresher ices, based mainly on sugar syrups with the addition of whisked egg whites to give a light consistency. They contain far fewer calories than custard- or cream-based ices, and are therefore particularly enjoyed by slimmers. They have been used for many years as a digestive during large gourmet banquets, usually being served between the fish course and the meat course, but nowadays such occasions are few and far between. However, savoury sorbets make extremely good summer starters and sweet sorbets are excellent to serve after a rich meal. Some sorbets will set without beating but, where recommended, beating the mixture during the freezing process will give the sorbet an even consistency and prevent any crystals forming (see page 4).

Sorbets take at least 5 hours' total freezing time and as with other ice creams they are best removed from the freezer to the refrigerator 45 minutes before serving.

Citrus sorbet

Metric	*Imperial*
grated rind and juice of	*grated rind and juice of*
2 oranges	*2 oranges*
grated rind and juice of	*grated rind and juice of*
1 lemon	*1 lemon*
grated rind and juice of	*grated rind and juice of*
1 grapefruit	*1 grapefruit*
water	*water*
100 g caster sugar	*4 oz caster sugar*
2 egg whites	*2 egg whites*

Preparation time: 15 minutes, plus freezing
Cooking time: about 8 minutes

Make the fruit juices up to 600 ml/1 pint with water.
Pour the liquid into a heavy-based saucepan and add
the grated fruit rinds and sugar. Heat gently until the
sugar has dissolved. Increase the heat and cook rapidly
until the thread stage is reached (see page 6). Allow
to cool.
Pour the mixture into a freezer container and, stirring
occasionally, freeze for about 1½ hours, until mushy.
Beat the egg whites until they form soft peaks. Fold
into the mixture and freeze. Beat the mixture three
times, at hourly intervals. Cover, seal and freeze.
Serves 4–6

Citrus sorbet; Chinese gooseberry sorbet

Chinese gooseberry sorbet

Metric	*Imperial*
600 ml water	*1 pint water*
2 × 15 ml spoons lemon	*2 tablespoons lemon*
juice	*juice*
100 g caster sugar	*4 oz caster sugar*
8 Chinese gooseberries,	*8 Chinese gooseberries,*
peeled	*peeled*
2 egg whites	*2 egg whites*

Preparation time: 20 minutes, plus freezing
Cooking time: about 8 minutes

Put the water, lemon juice and caster sugar into a
heavy-based saucepan. Heat gently until the sugar has
dissolved. Increase the heat and cook rapidly until the
thread stage is reached (see page 6). Allow to cool.
Liquidize or rub the Chinese gooseberries through a
nylon sieve using a wooden spoon. Stir the purée into
the sugar syrup.
Pour the mixture into a freezer container and, stirring
occasionally, freeze for about 1½ hours until mushy.
Beat the egg whites to form soft peaks. Fold into the
mixture and freeze. Beat once after 1 hour, then cover,
seal and freeze.
Serves 4–6

Cucumber sorbet

Metric
1 × 5 ml spoon gelatine
300 ml water
50 g sugar
juice of ½ lemon
1 large cucumber, peeled
  and cut into chunks
2 firm eating apples
1 × 5 ml spoon chopped
  fresh dill or 1 × 2.5 ml
  spoon dried dill weed
salt
freshly ground black
  pepper
2 egg whites

To serve:
6 prawns in their shells
fresh dill or parsley sprigs

Imperial
1 teaspoon gelatine
½ pint water
2 oz sugar
juice of ½ lemon
1 large cucumber, peeled
  and cut into chunks
2 firm eating apples
1 teaspoon chopped fresh
  dill or ½ teaspoon
  dried dill weed
salt
freshly ground black
  pepper
2 egg whites

To serve:
6 prawns in their shells
fresh dill or parsley sprigs

Preparation time: 25 minutes, plus freezing
Cooking time: 15 minutes

Scooped into tall glasses and garnished with prawns and sprigs of fresh dill or parsley this sorbet makes a temptingly light summer starter.

Put the gelatine and 2 × 15 ml spoons/2 tablespoons of the water in a small bowl and leave to soak.
Put the sugar and the remaining water in a heavy-based saucepan. Heat gently until the sugar has dissolved. Increase the heat and cook rapidly for 3 minutes. Allow to cool slightly, then pour the syrup over the gelatine and stir gently until the gelatine has completely dissolved. Stir in the lemon juice and allow to cool.
Peel and core the apples. Cut into chunks and liquidize with the cucumber and the sugar syrup. Add the dill, and salt and pepper to taste. Pour the mixture into a freezer container and, stirring occasionally, freeze for about 1½ hours until mushy.
Beat the egg whites until they form soft peaks and fold into the mixture. Cover, seal and freeze.
Serve garnished with the prawns in their shells and fresh dill or parsley.
Serves 6

Melon and mint sorbet

Metric
600 ml water
175 g caster sugar
1 × 15 ml spoon lemon
  juice
2 sprigs fresh mint,
  chopped
1 honeydew melon
1 × 5 ml spoon peppermint
  essence
2 egg whites

Imperial
1 pint water
6 oz caster sugar
1 tablespoon lemon
  juice
2 sprigs fresh mint,
  chopped
1 honeydew melon
1 teaspoon peppermint
  essence
2 egg whites

Preparation time: 20 minutes, plus freezing
Cooking time: about 8 minutes

The flavour of this sorbet will depend on the variety of fresh mint used. All are equally delicious and any type of melon can be used, too. The sorbet looks especially attractive scooped into glass dishes which have been lined with a few sprigs of mint.

Put the water, sugar and lemon juice in a heavy-based saucepan. Heat gently until the sugar has dissolved. Increase the heat and cook rapidly until the thread stage is reached (see page 6). Remove from the heat and stir in the chopped mint. Allow to cool.
Scoop the flesh from the melon, remove the pips and liquidize to a purée. Alternatively, rub through a nylon sieve using a wooden spoon. Stir into the sugar syrup with the peppermint essence. Pour the mixture into a freezer container and, stirring occasionally, freeze for about 1½ hours until mushy.
Beat the egg whites until they form soft peaks. Fold into the mixture and freeze. Beat the mixture twice, at hourly intervals. Cover, seal and freeze.
Serves 4–6

Clockwise from top: Cucumber sorbet; Tomato sorbet; Melon and mint sorbet

Tomato sorbet

Metric
100 g caster sugar
300 ml water
300 ml tomato juice
juice of ½ lemon
1 × 5 ml spoon
    Worcestershire sauce
6 drops Tabasco sauce
1 × 5 ml spoon soy sauce
salt
freshly ground black
    pepper
2 egg whites

To serve:
6 large ripe tomatoes
fresh coriander leaves
melba toast

Imperial
4 oz caster sugar
½ pint water
½ pint tomato juice
juice of ½ lemon
1 teaspoon
    Worcestershire sauce
6 drops Tabasco sauce
1 teaspoon soy sauce
salt
freshly ground black
    pepper
2 egg whites

To serve:
6 large ripe tomatoes
fresh coriander leaves
melba toast

Preparation time: 30 minutes, plus freezing
Cooking time: about 8 minutes

This makes an attractive starter served in Vandyke-style tomato halves cut with zig-zag edges.

Put the sugar and water in a heavy-based saucepan and heat gently until the sugar has dissolved. Increase the heat and cook rapidly until the thread stage is reached (see page 6). Allow to cool.
Stir in the tomato juice, lemon juice, Worcestershire, Tabasco and soy sauces. Add salt and pepper to taste. Pour into a freezer container and, stirring occasionally, freeze for about 1½ hours until mushy.
Beat the egg whites until they form soft peaks and fold into the tomato mixture. Cover, seal and freeze. To serve, allow the sorbet to defrost for about 45 minutes at room temperature. Halve the tomatoes with zigzag cuts, and scoop out the flesh and pips. Fill with scoops of the sorbet and garnish with sprigs of coriander. Serve with melba toast.
Makes 12 tomato halves

Pineapple colada sorbet

Metric
450 ml pineapple juice
300 ml water
100 g caster sugar
rind and juice of 1 lemon
50 g creamed coconut
2 egg whites

Imperial
¾ pint pineapple juice
½ pint water
4 oz caster sugar
rind and juice of 1 lemon
2 oz creamed coconut
2 egg whites

Preparation time: 15 minutes, plus freezing
Cooking time: about 8 minutes

For a special occasion this sorbet can be served in scooped-out pineapple halves. The fruit of the pineapple can then be chopped and used to decorate the finished dish.

Pour the pineapple juice and water into a heavy-based saucepan and add the sugar, lemon rind and lemon juice. Heat gently until the sugar has dissolved. Increase the heat and cook rapidly until the thread stage is reached (see page 6). Remove from the heat and immediately add the creamed coconut, stirring gently until it melts. Allow to cool.
Pour the mixture into a freezer container and, stirring occasionally, freeze for about 1½ hours until mushy. Beat the egg whites until they form soft peaks. Fold into the mixture and freeze. Beat the mixture twice, at hourly intervals. Cover, seal and freeze.
Serves 4–6

Pineapple colada sorbet; Lychee and lime sorbet;
Plum and gin sorbet

Lychee and lime sorbet

Metric
1 × 450 g can lychees
grated rind and juice of
    2 limes
water
100 g caster sugar
2 egg whites

Imperial
1 × 15 oz can lychees
grated rind and juice of
    2 limes
water
4 oz caster sugar
2 egg whites

Preparation time: 20 minutes, plus freezing
Cooking time: about 8 minutes

Drain the lychees and add the lime juice to the drained syrup. Make the liquid up to 600 ml/1 pint with water. Pour the liquid into a heavy-based saucepan and add the grated lime rind and sugar. Heat gently until the sugar has dissolved. Increase the heat and cook rapidly until the thread stage is reached (see page 6). Allow to cool.
Liquidize the lychees to a purée. Alternatively, rub through a nylon sieve using a wooden spoon. Pour the mixture into a freezer container and, stirring occasionally, freeze for about 1½ hours until mushy.
Beat the egg whites until they form soft peaks. Fold into the mixture and freeze. Beat once after 1 hour, then cover, seal and freeze.
Serves 4–6

Plum and gin sorbet

Metric
1 kg plums, halved and
    stoned
275 g caster sugar
750 ml water
2 × 15 ml spoons gin
2 egg whites

Imperial
2 lb plums, halved and
    stoned
10 oz caster sugar
1¼ pints water
2 tablespoons gin
2 egg whites

Preparation time: 20 minutes, plus freezing
Cooking time: 25 minutes

Put the plums into a saucepan with 100 g/4 oz of the
caster sugar and 150 ml/¼ pint of the water. Simmer
gently until the plums form a pulp. Rub through a
nylon sieve using a wooden spoon, to remove the
skins. Stir in the gin and allow to cool.
Put the remaining water and sugar in a heavy-based
saucepan. Heat gently until the sugar has dissolved.
Increase the heat and cook rapidly until the thread
stage is reached (see page 6). Allow to cool.
Stir the plum mixture into the sugar syrup. Pour the
mixture into a freezer container and, stirring occasionally, freeze for about 1½ hours until mushy.
Beat the egg whites until they form soft peaks. Fold
into the mixture and freeze. Beat the mixture twice,
at hourly intervals. Cover, seal and freeze.
Serves 4–6

Apple and sultana sorbet

Metric
600 ml still apple juice
50 g caster sugar
50 g sultanas
2 egg whites

Imperial
1 pint still apple juice
2 oz caster sugar
2 oz sultanas
2 egg whites

Preparation time: 15 minutes, plus freezing
Cooking time: about 8 minutes

Put the apple juice and sugar into a heavy-based saucepan. Heat gently until the sugar has dissolved. Increase the heat and cook rapidly until the thread stage is reached (see page 6). Stir in the sultanas and allow to cool.
Pour the mixture into a freezer container and, stirring occasionally, freeze for about 1½ hours until mushy. Beat the egg whites until they form soft peaks and fold into the mixture. Cover, seal and freeze.
Serves 4–6

Cherry sorbet

Metric
1 × 425 g can red cherries
water
175 g caster sugar
2 × 15 ml spoons cherry
  brandy
2 egg whites

Imperial
1 × 15 oz can red cherries
water
6 oz caster sugar
2 tablespoons cherry
  brandy
2 egg whites

Preparation time: 30 minutes, plus freezing
Cooking time: about 8 minutes

Drain the cherries and make the juice up to 600 ml/1 pint with water. Put the liquid and sugar into a heavy-based saucepan. Heat gently until the sugar has dissolved. Increase the heat and cook rapidly until the thread stage is reached (see page 6). Allow to cool.
Stone the cherries and liquidize or sieve them to a purée. Stir the purée into the cold syrup and add the cherry brandy.
Pour the mixture into a freezer container and, stirring occasionally, freeze for about 1½ hours until mushy. Beat the egg whites until they form soft peaks and fold into the cherry mixture. Cover, seal and freeze.
Serves 4–6

Blackcurrant sorbet

Metric
350 g fresh or frozen
  blackcurrants,
  topped and tailed
350 ml water
100 g caster sugar
2 × 5 ml spoons lemon
  juice
2 egg whites

Imperial
12 oz fresh or frozen
  blackcurrants,
  topped and tailed
12 fl oz water
4 oz caster sugar
2 teaspoons lemon
  juice
2 egg whites

Preparation time: 15 minutes, plus freezing
Cooking time: 25 minutes

Bottled or canned blackcurrants are a good alternative to fresh or frozen. Drain and cook then as directed.

Put the blackcurrants into a saucepan with 3 × 15 ml spoons/3 tablespoons of the water and simmer over a gentle heat until the fruit becomes pulpy. Rub through a nylon sieve using a wooden spoon.
Put the sugar and the remaining water in a heavy-based saucepan and gently heat until the sugar has dissolved. Increase the heat and cook rapidly until the syrup reaches the thread stage (see page 6). Allow to go cold.
Stir the syrup into the blackcurrant purée with the lemon juice. Pour the mixture into a freezer container and, stirring occasionally, freeze for about 1½ hours, until mushy.
Beat the egg whites until they form soft peaks. Fold into the blackcurrant mixture and freeze. Beat once after 1 hour, then cover, seal and freeze.
Serves 6

Variation:
Use redcurrants instead of blackcurrants.

Clockwise from top: Apple and sultana sorbet; Cherry sorbet; Blackcurrant sorbet

YOGURT-BASED ICE CREAM

Yogurt-based ice creams are much less rich than the custard- or cream-based varieties, and also contain far fewer calories. The flavour tends to be sharper and fresher, and the ices are reasonably inexpensive to prepare and popular with children. Flavoured yogurts of your choice may be used to replace the plain unsweetened yogurt, but the result will be a slightly sweeter ice cream.

Yogurt-based ice creams usually need beating during the freezing process (see page 4) and need a minimum of 3–4 hours' total freezing time. They are best removed from the freezer to the refrigerator 45 minutes before serving.

From left: Grapefruit and mint ice cream; Marmalade ice cream; Tangerine ice cream; Walnut tiles

Grapefruit and mint ice cream

Metric
2 grapefruits
100 g caster sugar
175 ml water
300 ml plain unsweetened
  yogurt
1 × 15 ml spoon chopped
  fresh mint
150 ml double or whipping
  cream

Imperial
2 grapefruits
4 oz caster sugar
6 fl oz water
10 fl oz plain unsweetened
  yogurt
1 tablespoon chopped
  fresh mint
5 fl oz double or whipping
  cream

Preparation time: 25 minutes, plus freezing
Cooking time: about 8 minutes

Cut the skin and pith from the grapefruit. Separate the segments, cutting them away from the membranes. Chop the segments finely, reserving any juice.
Put the sugar and water in a heavy-based saucepan and heat gently until the sugar has dissolved. Increase the heat and cook rapidly until the thread stage is reached (see page 6). Allow to cool.
Stir the chopped grapefruit, yogurt and mint into the syrup. Pour into a freezer container and freeze for about 1½ hours until mushy.
Beat the cream until it forms soft peaks. Fold into the mixture and freeze. Beat the mixture twice, at hourly intervals. Cover, seal and freeze.
Serves 6

Variation:
Use 4 oranges instead of the grapefruit, preparing the fruit in the same way.

Marmalade ice cream

Metric
100 g caster sugar
275 ml water
1 × 15 ml spoon lemon
  juice
4 × 15 ml spoons
  marmalade
300 ml plain unsweetened
  yogurt
150 ml double or whipping
  cream

Imperial
4 oz caster sugar
9 fl oz water
1 tablespoon lemon
  juice
4 tablespoons
  marmalade
10 fl oz plain unsweetened
  yogurt
5 fl oz double or whipping
  cream

Preparation time: 15 minutes, plus freezing
Cooking time: about 8 minutes

Put the sugar, water and lemon juice in a heavy-based saucepan and heat gently until the sugar has dissolved. Increase the heat and cook rapidly until the thread stage is reached (see page 6). Stir in the marmalade and allow to go cold.
Stir in the yogurt. Pour the mixture into a freezer container and freeze for about 1½ hours until mushy. Beat the cream until it forms soft peaks. Fold into the yogurt mixture and freeze. Beat the mixture twice, at hourly intervals. Cover, seal and freeze.
Serves 6

Tangerine ice cream

Metric
750 g tangerines, or
  oranges
50 g icing sugar, sifted
300 ml plain unsweetened
  yogurt
150 ml double cream

Imperial
1½ lb tangerines, or
  oranges
2 oz icing sugar, sifted
10 fl oz plain unsweetened
  yogurt
5 fl oz double cream

Preparation time: 25 minutes, plus freezing

Coarsely grate the rind of one of the tangerines or oranges. Squeeze the juice from the remaining fruit until about 300 ml/½ pint has been obtained.
Beat the icing sugar into the fruit juice and then slowly incorporate the yogurt. Pour into a freezer container and freeze for about 1½ hours until mushy. Beat the cream until it forms soft peaks. Beat into the frozen mixture with the grated rind and freeze. Beat the mixture twice, at hourly intervals. Cover, seal and freeze.
Serves 4–6

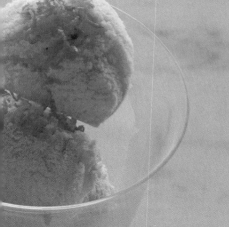

Muesli ice cream

Metric	Imperial
100 g caster sugar	*4 oz caster sugar*
300 ml water	*½ pint water*
100 g muesli	*4 oz muesli*
300 ml plain unsweetened yogurt	*10 fl oz plain unsweetened yogurt*
150 ml double or whipping cream	*5 fl oz double or whipping cream*

Preparation time: 15 minutes, plus freezing
Cooking time: about 8 minutes

Put the sugar and water into a heavy-based saucepan and gently heat until the sugar has dissolved. Increase the heat and cook rapidly until the thread stage is reached (see page 6). Allow to cool.
Stir the muesli into the yogurt, then stir in the syrup. Beat the cream until it forms soft peaks and fold into the mixture.
Pour into a freezer container and freeze. Beat the mixture twice, at hourly intervals. Cover, seal and freeze.
Serves 6

Strawberry and Kirsch ice cream

Metric	Imperial
100 g caster sugar	*4 oz caster sugar*
300 ml water	*½ pint water*
450 g fresh strawberries	*1 lb fresh strawberries*
1–2 × 15 ml spoons Kirsch	*1–2 tablespoons Kirsch*
300 ml plain unsweetened yogurt	*10 fl oz plain unsweetened yogurt*
150 ml double or whipping cream	*5 fl oz double or whipping cream*

Preparation time: 20 minutes, plus freezing
Cooking time: about 8 minutes

Put the sugar and water in a heavy-based saucepan and heat gently until the sugar has dissolved. Increase the heat and cook rapidly until the thread stage is reached (see page 6). Allow to cool.
Liquidize the strawberries with the Kirsch to a purée. Alternatively, rub them through a nylon sieve using a wooden spoon. Stir the yogurt and sugar syrup into the purée. Pour into a freezer container and freeze for about 1½ hours until mushy.
Beat the cream until it forms soft peaks. Fold into the strawberry mixture and freeze. Beat the mixture twice at hourly intervals. Cover, seal and freeze.
Serves 6

Pernod and peach ice cream

Metric	Imperial
4 fresh peaches	*4 fresh peaches*
100 g caster sugar	*4 oz caster sugar*
300 ml water	*½ pint water*
2 × 15 ml spoons Pernod	*2 tablespoons Pernod*
300 ml plain unsweetened yogurt	*10 fl oz plain unsweetened yogurt*
150 ml double or whipping cream	*5 fl oz double or whipping cream*

Preparation time: 20 minutes, plus freezing
Cooking time: about 8 minutes

With slices of fresh peaches and a little Pernod poured over the ice cream, this becomes an excellent dinner party dessert.

Put the peaches in a bowl and cover with boiling water. Drain after 15 seconds and remove the skins. Cut the peaches into quarters, discarding the stones. Put the sugar and water in a heavy-based saucepan and gently heat until the sugar has dissolved. Increase the heat and cook rapidly until the thread stage is reached (see page 6). Allow to cool.
Liquidize the syrup and the peaches together. Stir in the Pernod and the yogurt. Pour the mixture into a freezer container and freeze for about 1½ hours until it is mushy.
Beat the cream until it forms soft peaks. Fold into the peach mixture and freeze. Beat the mixture twice, at hourly intervals. Cover, seal and freeze.
Serves 6

From left: Strawberry ice cream; Pernod and peach ice cream; Muesli ice cream with melba sauce and sponge fingers

48

Rhubarb and ginger ice cream

Metric	*Imperial*
1 kg trimmed rhubarb, cut into 1 cm lengths	2 lb trimmed rhubarb, cut into ½ inch lengths
3 × 15 ml spoons water	3 tablespoons water
100 g caster sugar	4 oz caster sugar
300 ml plain unsweetened yogurt	10 fl oz plain unsweetened yogurt
50 g piece stem ginger, finely chopped	2 oz piece stem ginger, finely chopped
150 ml double or whipping cream	5 fl oz double or whipping cream

Preparation time: 15 minutes, plus freezing
Cooking time: 20 minutes

Put the rhubarb in a saucepan with the water and sugar. Cover and cook gently until soft. Cool.
Thoroughly mash the rhubarb with a fork, or use a liquidizer. Stir in the yogurt and chopped ginger. Beat the cream until it forms soft peaks, then fold into the rhubarb mixture.
Pour into a freezer container and freeze. Beat the mixture twice, at hourly intervals. Cover, seal and freeze.
Serves 6

Pineapple and parsley ice cream

Metric
750 g fresh pineapple
50 g icing sugar, sifted
300 ml plain unsweetened
  yogurt
1 × 15 ml spoon chopped
  fresh parsley
2 egg whites

Imperial
1½ lb fresh pineapple
2 oz icing sugar, sifted
10 fl oz plain unsweetened
  yogurt
1 tablespoon chopped
  fresh parsley
2 egg whites

Preparation time: 30 minutes, plus freezing

This makes an irresistible summer starter.

Remove the skin and core from the pineapple. Finely chop one-third of the flesh and set aside. Liquidize the remaining pineapple with the icing sugar and yogurt. Pour the purée into a freezer container and freeze for about 1½ hours until mushy.
Beat in the chopped pineapple and the parsley. Beat the egg whites until they form stiff peaks and fold into the pineapple mixture. Cover, seal and freeze.
Serves 6

Asparagus ice cream

Metric
2 × 350 g cans asparagus
  pieces, drained
2 × 15 ml spoons orange
  juice
3 × 15 ml spoons
  mayonnaise
250 ml plain unsweetened
  yogurt
salt
freshly ground black
  pepper
150 ml double or whipping
  cream

Imperial
2 × 12 oz cans asparagus
  pieces, drained
2 tablespoons orange
  juice
3 tablespoons
  mayonnaise
8 fl oz plain unsweetened
  yogurt
salt
freshly ground black
  pepper
5 fl oz double or whipping
  cream

To serve:
parsley sprigs
lemon wedges
fingers of toast

To serve:
parsley sprigs
lemon wedges
fingers of toast

Preparation time: 25 minutes, plus freezing

This is a refreshing ice cream to serve as a starter.

Liquidize or sieve the asparagus to a purée. Stir in the orange juice, mayonnaise and yogurt, and add salt and pepper to taste. Pour into a freezer container and freeze for about 1½ hours until mushy.
Beat the cream until it forms soft peaks. Fold into the asparagus mixture and freeze. Beat the mixture twice, at hourly intervals. Cover, seal and freeze.
Serve as a starter, garnished with parsley sprigs and lemon wedges, and accompanied by fingers of toast.
Serves 6

Rhubarb and ginger ice cream; Pineapple and parsley ice cream; Asparagus ice cream with cheese fingers

ACCOMPANYING BISCUITS

These recipes give some exciting ideas for
attractive biscuits to serve with all types of ice
cream. All the biscuits may be made in advance
if carefully stored, and add a delightful contrast
in texture to the ice creams themselves. Store
the biscuits in sealed plastic containers for 3–4
days. They should not be kept in a freezer.

Puff pastry and nut twirls

Metric	*Imperial*
1 × 215 g packet puff pastry	*1 × 7½ oz packet puff pastry*
1 egg white, lightly beaten	*1 egg white, lightly beaten*
25 g caster sugar	*1 oz caster sugar*
50 g blanched almonds, finely chopped	*2 oz blanched almonds, finely chopped*
icing sugar, to serve	*icing sugar, to serve*

Preparation time: 15 minutes
Cooking time: 8–10 minutes
Oven: 230°C, 450°F, Gas Mark 8

Roll out the pastry to a 30 × 20 cm/12 × 8 inch
rectangle. Brush half the length of the surface with the
lightly beaten egg white, then sprinkle this half with
the sugar and the chopped almonds. Press the nuts
and sugar gently into the surface with the back of the
hand. Fold the pastry over lengthwise, then gently
roll to seal. Cut into strips, twisting each one, and
place on a dampened baking tray.
Bake in a preheated oven for 8–10 minutes, or until
the twists are puffed and light golden brown in colour.
Leave to cool on a wire tray. Serve dusted with a little
sifted icing sugar.
Makes 20

Puff pastry and nut twirls; Brandy and sultana biscuits;
Ginger snaps

Brandy and sultana biscuits

Metric	*Imperial*
50 g sultanas, washed and drained	2 oz sultanas, washed and drained
water	water
2 × 15 ml spoons brandy	2 tablespoons brandy
2 eggs	2 eggs
1 egg yolk	1 egg yolk
50 g caster sugar	2 oz caster sugar
165 g plain flour, sifted	5½ oz plain flour, sifted
2 × 15 ml spoons double or whipping cream	2 tablespoons double or whipping cream

Preparation time: 20 minutes
Cooking time: 10–15 minutes
Oven: 190°C, 375°F, Gas Mark 5

Put the sultanas in a saucepan with a little water and bring to just below boiling point. Drain and place in a small bowl with the brandy. Set the sultanas and brandy to one side.

Put the eggs and the extra yolk in a bowl with the sugar and beat them together until the mixture is pale in colour. Add the sifted flour and cream and mix well.

Lightly grease 2 baking trays. Drop the mixture in small spoonfuls on to the trays. Flatten the biscuits with a wet fork and place a few of the brandy-flavoured sultanas in the centre of each.

Bake in a preheated oven for 10–15 minutes, or until golden brown round the edges. Allow to cool slightly before placing the biscuits on a wire tray.
Makes 20

Ginger snaps

Metric	*Imperial*
50 g golden syrup	2 oz golden syrup
50 g butter	2 oz butter
150 g caster sugar	5 oz caster sugar
50 g plain flour, sifted	2 oz plain flour, sifted
1 × 5 ml spoon ground ginger	1 teaspoon ground ginger
1 × 2.5 ml spoon grated lemon rind	½ teaspoon grated lemon rind
1 × 2.5 ml spoon lemon juice	½ teaspoon lemon juice

Preparation time: 25 minutes
Cooking time: 35–50 minutes
Oven: 180°C, 350°F, Gas Mark 4

This mixture makes delicious Ginger Coupelles (see page 58 for fillings). Set the biscuits around the bottom halves of oranges or apples, or ramekin dishes or dariole moulds.

Bake 3 biscuits at a time so that they can be moulded into shape before they set hard. Because each batch of biscuits needs to be cooked on a cool baking tray it is a good idea to have 3 trays in use.

Put the syrup, butter and sugar in a saucepan and stir over a gentle heat until the sugar has dissolved. Remove from the heat. Fold in the sifted flour, ground ginger, lemon rind and lemon juice.

Lightly grease 3 baking trays. Drop 3 small spoonfuls of the mixture on to a tray, leaving plenty of room for the biscuits to spread. Bake in a preheated oven for 7–10 minutes or until golden in colour.

Quickly remove the ginger snaps from the baking tray and shape them by winding around the handles of wooden spoons. When set, remove from the spoons and cool on trays.

Cook the remaining biscuits similarly, using a cool baking tray for each batch. Shape and allow the biscuits to go cold.
Makes 14

Walnut tiles

Metric	Imperial
50 g butter	2 oz butter
2 egg whites	2 egg whites
65 g caster sugar	2½ oz caster sugar
50 g plain flour, sifted	2 oz plain flour, sifted
25 g walnut halves, coarsely chopped	1 oz walnut halves, coarsely chopped
a little icing sugar, sifted	a little icing sugar, sifted

Preparation time: 15 minutes
Cooking time: about 30 minutes
Oven: 200 °C, 400 °F, Gas Mark 6

As these biscuits will set hard in about 1 minute, it is advisable to cook and shape only 3 or 4 at a time. Because they need to be cooked on cool baking trays each time it is a good idea to have 3 trays in use.

Melt the butter gently over a low heat and cool. Beat the egg whites until frothy, then add the caster sugar and beat for 2–3 minutes until the mixture thickens. Gently fold in the sifted flour together with the melted butter and chopped walnuts.
Lightly grease 3 baking trays. Drop 3 or 4 small spoonfuls of the mixture on to a tray. Spread each biscuit into a shallow circle. Dust with a little sifted icing sugar and bake in a preheated oven for about 5 minutes, or until golden brown round the edges.
Carefully remove the biscuits from the trays and place on a lightly greased rolling pin, pressing gently with the hands to make the tile shape. When set, allow to go cold on a wire tray.
Cook the remaining biscuits similarly, using a cool baking tray for each batch.
Makes 20

Variation:
Chopped hazelnuts or flaked almonds may be substituted for the walnuts.

Cheese fingers

Metric	Imperial
100 g plain flour	4 oz plain flour
1 × 2.5 ml spoon salt	½ teaspoon salt
100 g chilled butter, chopped	4 oz chilled butter, chopped
75 g Cheddar cheese, finely grated	3 oz Cheddar cheese, finely grated
25 g grated Parmesan cheese	1 oz grated Parmesan cheese
pinch of cayenne pepper	pinch of cayenne pepper
about 1 × 15 ml spoon water	about 1 tablespoon water

Preparation time: 15 minutes
Cooking time: 7–10 minutes
Oven: 160°C, 325°F, Gas Mark 3

Serve these fingers either hot or cold with any of the more savoury ice creams.

Sift the flour and salt into a mixing bowl and add the butter. Rub the butter into the flour until the mixture resembles fine breadcrumbs. Stir in the Cheddar cheese, Parmesan, and cayenne pepper. Using a round-bladed knife, stir in enough cold water to form a stiff dough.
Turn the dough on to a floured board and knead. Roll out to a thickness of 5 mm/¼ inch and cut into 7.5 × 1 cm/3 × ½ inch fingers.
Arrange the fingers on a greased baking tray and bake in a preheated oven for 7–10 minutes until crisp and lightly browned.
Makes 24

Walnut tiles; Chinese fingers; Shortbread biscuits

Shortbread biscuits

Metric	*Imperial*
225 g plain flour	*8 oz plain flour*
225 g self-raising flour	*8 oz self-raising flour*
225 g butter	*8 oz butter*
100 g caster sugar	*4 oz caster sugar*
pinch of salt	*pinch of salt*

Preparation time: 25 minutes
Cooking time: about 45 minutes
Oven: 160°C, 325°F, Gas Mark 3

Sift the plain and self-raising flour into a bowl. Cream the butter and sugar together in a separate bowl until pale and light in colour. Gently stir in the sifted flour and the salt, and mix to a light dough.
Turn the dough on to a lightly floured pastry board and divide into 2 halves. Form each half into a circle 5 mm/$\frac{1}{4}$ inch thick by pressing with the hands. Do not knead or roll the mixture as it will lose its shortness. Place the rounds on a lightly greased baking tray. Pinch the edges with finger and thumb and prick the surface with a fork. Bake in a preheated oven for about 45 minutes.
Cut each circle into 8 wedges. Cool on a wire tray.
Makes 16

Variation:
50 g/2 oz chopped almonds, hazelnuts or walnuts may be added to the shortbread with the flour.

Langues de chat

Metric	Imperial
50 g butter	2 oz butter
50 g caster sugar	2 oz caster sugar
2 egg whites	2 egg whites
50 g plain flour, sifted	2 oz plain flour, sifted

Preparation time: 20 minutes
Cooking time: 4–5 minutes
Oven: 220°C, 425°F, Gas Mark 7

Cream the butter with a wooden spoon for 2–3 minutes. Beat in the caster sugar and continue beating until the mixture is light and fluffy. Gradually beat the egg whites into the mixture, then gently fold in the sifted flour.

Lightly grease and flour a baking tray. Using a forcing bag with a plain 1 cm/½ inch nozzle, pipe the mixture on to the baking tray in finger lengths. Leave 2.5 cm/1 inch space between the biscuits to allow them to spread during baking.

Bake in a preheated oven for 4–5 minutes until tinged with brown around the edges. Carefully remove the biscuits from the baking tray and place on a wire tray to cool.

Makes 18–20

Orange and almond galettes

Metric	Imperial
65 g butter, softened	2½ oz butter, softened
90 g caster sugar	3½ oz caster sugar
75 g chopped almonds	3 oz chopped almonds
75 g candied orange peel, chopped	3 oz candied orange peel, chopped
40 g plain flour, sifted	1½ oz plain flour, sifted
2 × 5 ml spoons milk	2 teaspoons milk

Preparation time: 15 minutes
Cooking time: 5–7 minutes
Oven: 220°C, 425°F, Gas Mark 7

Cream the butter and sugar together, beating well with a wooden spoon for 2–3 minutes. Stir in the almonds and the chopped candied orange peel, then the sifted flour and milk.

Place the mixture in small spoonfuls 5 cm/2 inches apart on a lightly greased baking tray. Flatten each spoonful gently with a wet fork. Bake in a preheated oven for 5–7 minutes.

Allow the biscuits to cool on the baking tray for 3–4 minutes before removing to a wire tray.

Makes 18–20

Langues de chat; Orange and almond galettes; Chocolate sablés; Sponge finger biscuits

Chocolate sablés

Metric	Imperial
120 g plain flour	4½ oz plain flour
40 g caster sugar	1½ oz caster sugar
65 g butter	2½ oz butter
2 egg yolks	2 egg yolks
1 × 5 ml spoon grated orange rind	1 teaspoon grated orange rind
100 g plain chocolate	4 oz plain chocolate

Preparation time: 35 minutes
Cooking time: about 15 minutes
Oven: 190°C, 375°F, Gas Mark 5

Sift the flour into a basin or on to a pastry board and make a well in the centre. Put the sugar, butter, egg yolks and grated orange rind in the well and work the mixture together with the fingertips until it forms a dough.

Knead lightly, then roll out on a lightly floured surface to 5 mm/¼ inch thickness. Cut out rounds using a 5 cm/2 inch fluted cutter and place on a lightly greased baking tray. Bake in a preheated oven for 10–15 minutes. Cool on a wire tray.

Melt the chocolate in a small bowl over a pan of hot water. When the biscuits are cold spread the top of each with chocolate and make a pattern with a fork.
Makes 20

Sponge finger biscuits

Metric	Imperial
3 eggs, separated	3 eggs, separated
75 g caster sugar	3 oz caster sugar
90 g plain flour, sifted	3½ oz plain flour, sifted
2 drops vanilla essence	2 drops vanilla essence
icing sugar, sifted	icing sugar, sifted

Preparation time: 30 minutes
Cooking time: 10–12 minutes
Oven: 180°C, 350°F, Gas Mark 4

Line 2 baking trays with lightly greased greaseproof paper and set aside. Place the egg yolks and sugar in a bowl and cream together thoroughly until thick and pale in colour.

Beat the egg whites stiffly and fold into the yolk mixture together with the sifted flour and vanilla essence. Spoon the mixture into a forcing bag fitted with a plain 1 cm/½ inch nozzle. Pipe into finger lengths on the greaseproof paper. Dust with sifted icing sugar and bake in a preheated oven for 10–12 minutes. When cooked, carefully remove the paper and allow the biscuits to cool on a wire tray.
Makes 20

Variation:
When cold, the ends of the biscuits may be dipped in melted chocolate.

Plain coupelles

Metric	*Imperial*
50 g butter	*2 oz butter*
2 egg whites	*2 egg whites*
65 g caster sugar	*2½ oz caster sugar*
50 g plain flour, sifted	*2 oz plain flour, sifted*

Preparation time: 15 minutes
Cooking time: 20–25 minutes
Oven: 200°C, 400°F, Gas Mark 6

Coupelles are brittle and should be stored carefully in tins or plastic containers. For filling and serving them see right. As the cooked biscuits will set hard within 2 minutes it is advisable to bake only 3 biscuits at a time but because each batch should be baked on a cool baking tray it is best to use 3 trays in rotation.

Melt the butter gently over a low heat, and allow to cool. Beat the egg whites until frothy, add the caster sugar and beat for 2–3 minutes until thick. Gently fold in the sifted flour together with the melted butter. Lightly grease 3 baking trays. Drop 3 spoonfuls of the mixture on to a tray and spread each spoonful out to form a circle 10 cm/4 inches in diameter. Bake in a preheated oven for 5–7 minutes or until the edges are a light golden brown.

Carefully remove the biscuits from the baking tray and quickly shape round the bottom half of an orange or apple, or a ramekin dish. When set in shape, remove from the moulds and leave to go completely cold on a wire tray.

Cook the remaining biscuits similarly, using a cool baking tray for each batch. Shape and allow the biscuits to go cold.

Makes 8–10

Plain and ginger coupelles with fillings; Russian cigar biscuits

Coupelle fillings

Served on small plates or in wide-necked glasses, coupelles make an impressive dinner party sweet. With biscuit mixture made from the Plain Coupelles (see left) or the Ginger Snaps (page 53), any of the ice creams may be used as a filling. However the following are some suggestions. One recipe quantity of ice cream should fill 6 coupelles.

Remove the ice cream from the freezer and allow it to defrost in the refrigerator for about 45 minutes before using. Then scoop it into the biscuit shapes just before serving, to prevent the biscuits from becoming soft.

Plain Coupelles

1. Fill with scoops of Grape Ice Cream (page 37) and scatter with peeled and halved black and white grapes.
2. Fill with scoops of Strawberry Ice Cream (page 27) and pipe whirls of whipped cream on top. Sprinkle with toasted flaked almonds.
3. Fill with scoops of Chestnut and Chocolate Ripple (page 10) and decorate with grated chocolate.

Ginger Coupelles

4. Fill with scoops of Basic Vanilla Ice Cream (page 8) and pour over Redcurrant Syrup (page 24). Sprinkle with chopped hazelnuts.
5. Fill with scoops of Cranberry Ice Cream (page 32) and decorate with orange twists.

Russian cigar biscuits

Metric
40 g butter
2 egg whites
65 g caster sugar
50 g plain flour, sifted
1 × 15 ml spoon ground
  almonds

Imperial
1½ oz butter
2 egg whites
2½ oz caster sugar
2 oz plain flour, sifted
1 tablespoon ground
  almonds

Preparation time: 15 minutes
Cooking time: about 30 minutes
Oven: 200°C, 400°F, Gas Mark 6

It is advisable to cook only 3 of these biscuits at a time as speed is needed in shaping them. However the mixture has to be spread on to cool trays, so it is a good idea to have 3 trays in use.

Melt the butter gently over a low heat, and allow to cool. Beat the egg whites until frothy, add the caster sugar and beat again for 2–3 minutes until the mixture is thick. Gently fold in the sifted flour together with the melted butter and the ground almonds.
Lightly grease 3 baking trays. Drop 3 small spoonfuls of the mixture on to a tray. Spread each spoonful into a shallow oval shape and bake in a preheated oven for about 5 minutes, or until the biscuits are lightly browned round the edges.
Quickly remove the biscuits from the baking tray and curl them round the handle of a wooden spoon while still hot. Allow the biscuits to set in shape for 2–3 minutes before removing to a wire tray to go completely cold.
Cook the remaining biscuits similarly, using a cool baking tray for each batch. Curl and allow the biscuits to set in shape.
Makes 15–18

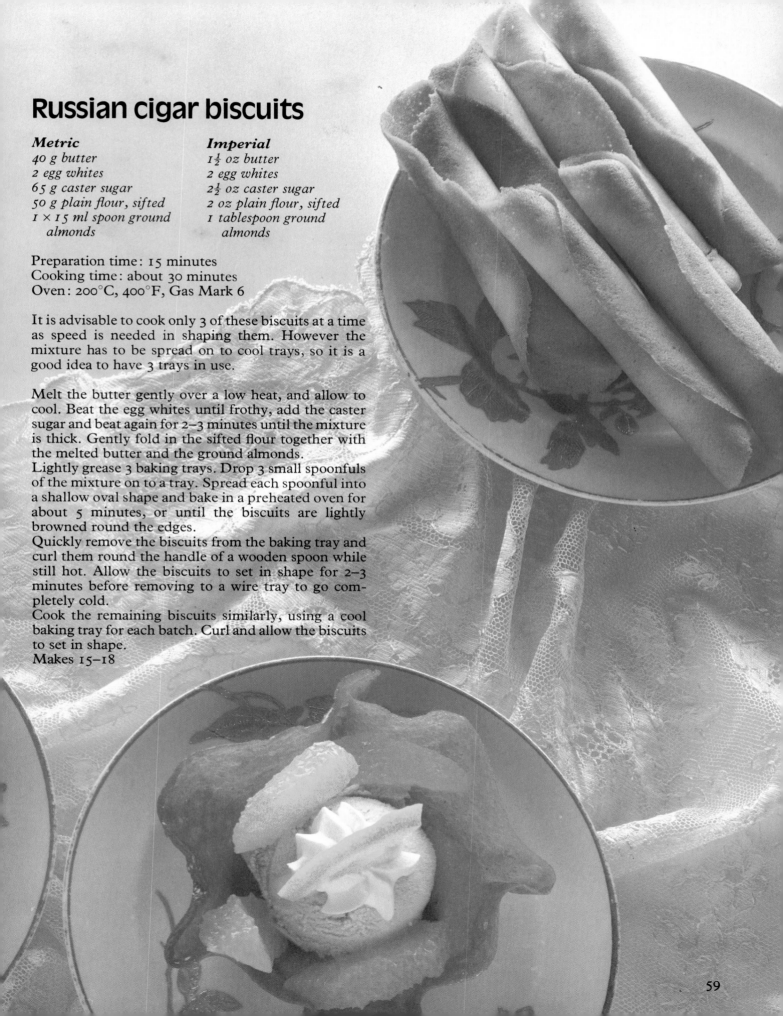

SPECIAL OCCASIONS

The recipes in this chapter suggest various ways of using ice cream to make impressive sweets for special occasions. The basic cakes and meringue bases can be made in advance, and stored according to the instructions in the recipes. Then the actual assembly of the sweets takes very little time.

The Genoese-based ice cream cakes can be layered with the ice cream and frozen until required. They should be wrapped in foil, sealed and placed in the freezer for up to 3 months. Before decorating and serving, the ice cream cakes should be unwrapped and defrosted for about 45 minutes in the refrigerator. This gives the cake just time to thaw, without allowing the ice cream to become too soft.

So that the ice creams are easy to work with they are sometimes defrosted at room temperature in this chapter.

Genoese sponge cake

Metric
4 eggs
120 g caster sugar
90 g plain flour, sifted
90 g unsalted butter,
  melted and cooled
1 × 5 ml spoon grated
  lemon rind

Imperial
4 eggs
4½ oz caster sugar
3½ oz plain flour, sifted
3½ oz unsalted butter,
  melted and cooled
1 teaspoon grated lemon
  rind

Preparation time: 20 minutes
Cooking time: 25–30 minutes
Oven: 180°C, 350°F, Gas Mark 4

Break the eggs into a bowl and add the sugar. Using an electric mixer, beat the eggs and sugar together for about 8 minutes until thick and creamy and double in volume. Alternatively beat the mixture by hand over a saucepan of hot water. Gradually fold in the flour and melted butter. Stir in the lemon rind.
Spoon the mixture into a greased and floured baking tin (see individual recipes in this chapter for size). Bake in a preheated oven for 25–30 minutes. When cooked, leave the cake in the tin for 5 minutes before turning out on to a wire tray to cool.
Store in an airtight container for 2–3 days, or freeze for up to 4 months.

Rum and raisin cake

Rum and raisin cake

Metric
1 quantity Genoese Sponge
  Cake (see left), baked
  in an 18 × 28 cm
  battenburg tin
1 quantity Rum and
  Raisin Ice Cream
  (page 11)

Imperial
1 quantity Genoese Sponge
  Cake (see left), baked
  in a 7 × 11 inch
  battenburg tin
1 quantity Rum and
  Raisin Ice Cream
  (page 11)

To decorate:
450 ml double or whipping
  cream, whipped
100 g black grapes, halved
  and seeded
100 g white grapes, halved
  and seeded

To decorate:
15 fl oz double or whipping
  cream, whipped
4 oz black grapes, halved
  and seeded
4 oz white grapes, halved
  and seeded

Preparation time: 20 minutes, plus softening and chilling

Remove the rum and raisin ice cream from the freezer and allow to soften slightly for about 25 minutes at room temperature.
With a sharp knife carefully cut the sponge cake in half horizontally and sandwich together with the rum and raisin ice cream.
To serve, cover the cake completely with whipped cream and decorate with black and white grapes in an alternating pattern. Place the cake in the freezer for 15 minutes to chill before serving.
Serves 8

Caramel and blackcurrant cake

Metric

1 quantity Genoese Sponge Cake (page 61), baked in a 20 cm sandwich tin
1 quantity Caramel Ice Cream (page 28)
1 quantity Blackcurrant Ice Cream (page 33)

To decorate:
250 ml double or whipping cream
1 × 5 ml spoon caster sugar
1 drop vanilla essence
50 g nibbed nuts, toasted

Imperial

1 quantity Genoese Sponge Cake (page 61), baked in an 8 inch sandwich tin
1 quantity Caramel Ice Cream (page 28)
1 quantity Blackcurrant Ice Cream (page 33)

To decorate:
8 fl oz double or whipping cream
1 teaspoon caster sugar
1 drop vanilla essence
2 oz nibbed nuts, toasted

Preparation time: 20 minutes, plus softening and chilling

Remove the caramel and blackcurrant ice creams from the freezer and allow to soften slightly for about 25 minutes at room temperature.

With a sharp knife carefully cut the sponge cake horizontally into 3 layers. Sandwich together, filling one layer with caramel ice cream and one layer with blackcurrant ice cream.

To serve, beat the cream until it forms soft peaks. Fold in the sugar and vanilla essence. Cover the cake roughly with the cream, forming soft peaks all over. Decorate with the nuts and chill for 15 minutes in the freezer before serving.

Serves 6–8

Black cherry gâteau

Metric
1 quantity Black Cherry
  Ice Cream (page 13)
1 quantity Genoese Sponge
  Cake (page 61), baked
  in a 15 cm round tin

To decorate:
175 ml double or whipping
  cream, whipped
150 ml Black Cherry
  Syrup (page 19)

Imperial
1 quantity Black Cherry
  Ice Cream (page 13)
1 quantity Genoese Sponge
  Cake (page 61), baked
  in a 6 inch round tin

To decorate:
6 fl oz double or whipping
  cream, whipped
5 fl oz Black Cherry
  Syrup (page 19)

Preparation time: 20 minutes, plus softening and chilling

Remove the black cherry ice cream from the freezer and allow to soften slightly for about 25 minutes at room temperature.
Turn the sponge cake upside down and cut a shallow circle out of the base, to within 1 cm/½ inch of the edge. Set the circle to one side, taking care not to damage it. Hollow out the cake deeply to make a container for the ice cream (the crumbs can be stored in the freezer for use in trifles).
Pack the black cherry ice cream firmly into the hollowed-out cake and cover with the reserved circle of cake. Transfer the cake to a serving plate.
To serve, decorate by piping rosettes of whipped cream over the surface. Dribble black cherry syrup over the top and chill for 15 minutes in the freezer before serving.
Serves 6–8

Old-fashioned peach melba

Metric
1 quantity Basic Vanilla
  Ice Cream (page 8)
4 peaches
2 × 15 ml spoons Kirsch
150 ml Melba Sauce
  (page 19)
120 ml double or whipping
  cream, lightly whipped
50 g chopped almonds,
  toasted

Imperial
1 quantity Basic Vanilla
  Ice Cream (page 8)
4 peaches
2 tablespoons Kirsch
¼ pint Melba Sauce
  (page 19)
4 fl oz double or whipping
  cream, lightly whipped
2 oz chopped almonds,
  toasted

Preparation time: 30 minutes, plus softening and soaking

Peach melbas are said to have been originally prepared by a Melbourne chef in honour of the singer Dame Nelli Melba.

Remove the ice creams from the freezer and allow to soften in the refrigerator for 45 minutes. Meanwhile skin the peaches by pouring boiling water over them and leave to stand for 10 seconds. Drain off the water. The skins should now peel easily away.
Cut each peach in half and remove the stones. Put the peach halves in a large bowl and pour over the Kirsch. Leave to soak for 15 minutes, turning occasionally.
To assemble the peach melba, drain the Kirsch and add it to the melba sauce. Sandwich each pair of peach halves together with generous scoops of the softened vanilla ice cream and put on individual plates. Pour over the sauce and top each serving with a spoonful of whipped cream. Sprinkle with nuts and serve immediately.
Serves 4

Caramel and blackcurrant cake; Black cherry gâteau; Old-fashioned peach melba

Pastry meringue cake

Metric
150 g plain flour
75 g butter, cut into pieces
50 g caster sugar
2 egg yolks

Imperial
5 oz plain flour
3 oz butter, cut into pieces
2 oz caster sugar
2 egg yolks

Meringue:
3 egg whites
175 g caster sugar

Meringue:
3 egg whites
6 oz caster sugar

Preparation time: 40 minutes, plus chilling
Cooking time: 1–1½ hours
Oven: 180°C, 350°F, Gas Mark 4;
     150°C, 300°F, Gas Mark 2

As a basis for a dessert this meringue cake is very adaptable. Many combinations of ice creams can be scooped in the centre. Choose those which both taste and look good together.

Sift the flour into a basin or on to a pastry board and make a well in the centre. Put the butter, sugar and egg yolks in the well and work the mixture together with the fingertips until it forms a dough. Knead lightly, then chill in the refrigerator for 20 minutes. Roll out the pastry to form a 20 cm/8 inch circle and place on a lightly greased baking tray. Prick the pastry with a fork and bake in a preheated oven for 20–25 minutes, or until golden brown. Remove from the oven and set the pastry aside to cool. Reduce the oven temperature.
To make the meringue, beat the egg whites until very stiff and they can be cut through with a knife. Whisk in 2 × 15 ml spoons/2 tablespoons of the caster sugar and then gently fold in the remainder.
Spoon the meringue mixture into a large forcing bag fitted with a large rose nozzle and pipe round the edge of the pastry base. Return the pastry meringue cake to the cooled oven and bake for 45 minutes–1 hour to set the meringue. Cool on a wire tray.
Store in an airtight container for up to 3 days, or freeze for up to 3 months.

Grape meringue cake

Metric
1 quantity Grape Ice
  Cream (page 37)
1 quantity Melon and
  Ginger Ice Cream
  (page 37)
1 Pastry Meringue Cake
  (see left)

Imperial
1 quantity Grape Ice
  Cream (page 37)
1 quantity Melon and
  Ginger Ice Cream
  (page 37)
1 Pastry Meringue Cake
  (see left)

To decorate:
50 g white grapes, seeded
50 g black grapes, seeded
melon balls
85 ml Orange Syrup
  (page 24)

To decorate:
2 oz white grapes, seeded
2 oz black grapes, seeded
melon balls
3 fl oz Orange Syrup
  (page 24)

Preparation time: 20 minutes, plus softening

Remove the ice creams from the freezer and allow to soften in the refrigerator for 45 minutes. Put the pastry meringue base on a serving plate and fill the centre with alternate scoops of the ice creams. Decorate with whole, seeded grapes and melon balls. Dribble the orange syrup over the top and serve immediately.
Serves 8–10

Strawberry meringue cake

Metric
1 quantity Sweet
  Peppermint Ice Cream
  (page 33)
1 quantity Strawberry
  Ice Cream (page 27)
1 Pastry Meringue Cake
  (see left)

Imperial
1 quantity Sweet
  Peppermint Ice Cream
  (page 33)
1 quantity Strawberry
  Ice Cream (page 27)
1 Pastry Meringue Cake
  (see left)

To decorate:
50 g flaked almonds,
  toasted
100 g strawberries
6 sprigs fresh mint

To decorate:
2 oz flaked almonds,
  toasted
4 oz strawberries
6 sprigs fresh mint

Preparation time: 15 minutes, plus softening

Remove the ice creams from the freezer and allow to soften in the refrigerator for 45 minutes. Put the pastry meringue base on a serving plate and fill the centre with alternate scoops of the ice creams.
Sprinkle with toasted almonds and decorate with strawberries and mint sprigs. Serve immediately.
Serves 8–10

Grape meringue cake; Strawberry meringue cake

Muesli banana splits

Metric
1 quantity Muesli Ice
  Cream (page 48)
4 bananas
150 ml Orange Syrup
  (page 24)
50 g sultanas
grated orange rind,
  to decorate

Imperial
1 quantity Muesli Ice
  Cream (page 48)
4 bananas
¼ pint Orange Syrup
  (page 24)
2 oz sultanas
grated orange rind,
  to decorate

Preparation time: 10 minutes, plus softening

Experiment with your own choice of ice cream and syrup.

Remove the ice cream from the freezer and allow it to soften in the refrigerator for 45 minutes. Peel the bananas and split them lengthwise. Sandwich the halves together with the softened muesli ice cream. Place each filled banana in a separate serving dish. Drizzle over the orange syrup, sprinkle with sultanas and top each split with an orange twist. Serve immediately.
Serves 4

Crystallized fruit cake

Metric
25 g angelica, finely
 chopped
50 g stoned raisins
50 g mixed peel
2 × 15 ml spoons port
1 quantity Basic Vanilla
 Ice Cream (page 8)
50 g blanched almonds,
 chopped

Imperial
1 oz angelica, finely
 chopped
2 oz stoned raisins
2 oz mixed peel
2 tablespoons port
1 quantity Basic Vanilla
 Ice Cream (page 8)
2 oz blanched almonds,
 chopped

Cake:
150 ml egg whites
1 × 2.5 ml spoon cream of
 tartar
pinch of salt
50 g plain flour, sifted
 3 times
150 g caster sugar

Cake:
5 fl oz egg whites
½ teaspoon cream of
 tartar
pinch of salt
2 oz plain flour, sifted
 3 times
5 oz caster sugar

To decorate:
75 g caster sugar
4 × 15 ml spoons water
50 g flaked almonds,
 toasted

To decorate:
3 oz caster sugar
4 tablespoons water
2 oz flaked almonds,
 toasted

Muesli banana splits; Crystallized fruit cake

Preparation time: 40 minutes, plus soaking, cooling
and softening
Cooking time: about 1 hour
Oven: 140°C, 275°F, Gas Mark 1;
    160°C, 325°F, Gas Mark 3

Put the angelica, raisins, mixed peel and port into a
bowl and leave to soak for 2–3 hours.
Remove the vanilla ice cream from the freezer and
allow to soften in the refrigerator for about 20 minutes.
Stir the almonds and soaked fruit gently into the
softened ice cream. Cover and return to the freezer.
To make the cake, pour the egg whites into a large
bowl and beat until frothy. Sprinkle the cream of
tartar and salt into the bowl and continue beating until
the egg whites form very stiff peaks. Fold the flour and
sugar carefully into the egg whites, a little at a time.
Spoon the mixture into a well-greased 15 cm/6 inch
round cake tin.
Bake in a preheated oven for 40 minutes. Increase the
heat and bake for a further 10 minutes. The cake is
cooked when the sides have slightly shrunk away from
the tin. Remove from the oven and allow to stand in
the tin for 30 minutes. Turn out on to a wire tray and
leave to go completely cold.
To assemble the ice cream cake, remove the ice cream
mixture from the freezer and allow to soften slightly
for about 25 minutes at room temperature. Cut the
cake horizontally into 4 layers and sandwich together
with the ice cream.
To decorate, put the sugar and water in a heavy-based
saucepan and gently heat until the sugar has dissolved.
Increase the heat and cook rapidly until the thread
stage is reached (see page 6). Remove from the heat
and stir in the toasted almonds, coating them
thoroughly in syrup. Allow to cool slightly. Remove
the coated almonds with a slotted draining spoon and
use to decorate the top of the cake. Dribble the
slightly cooled syrup over and serve immediately.
Serves 6

Sweet peppermint and chocolate Swiss roll

Metric	Imperial
75 g plain flour	*3 oz plain flour*
pinch of salt	*pinch of salt*
1 × 5 ml spoon baking powder	*1 teaspoon baking powder*
3 eggs	*3 eggs*
100 g caster sugar	*4 oz caster sugar*
1 quantity Chocolate and Orange Ice Cream (page 10)	*1 quantity Chocolate and Orange Ice Cream (page 10)*
1 quantity Sweet Peppermint Ice Cream (page 33)	*1 quantity Sweet Peppermint Ice Cream (page 33)*
50 g chocolate polka dots	*2 oz chocolate polka dots*

To decorate:	**To decorate:**
300 ml double or whipping cream, whipped	*10 fl oz double or whipping cream, whipped*
50 g plain chocolate, grated	*2 oz plain chocolate, grated*

Preparation time: 40 minutes, plus overnight standing, softening and chilling
Cooling time: 8 minutes
Oven: 190°C, 375°F, Gas Mark 5

Grease a 23 × 33 cm/9 × 13 inch Swiss roll tin and line it with lightly oiled greaseproof paper.
Sift the plain flour, salt and baking powder into a bowl. Using an electric mixer, beat the eggs and 75 g/3 oz of the sugar together in a bowl until thick and pale. Gradually fold in the dry, sifted ingredients and spoon the mixture into the prepared tin. Spread evenly over the tin and into the corners. Bake in a preheated oven for 8 minutes.
Meanwhile, lay a sheet of greaseproof paper on a warm, dampened tea towel. Dredge the paper evenly with the remaining caster sugar. When the cake is cooked, turn it out on to the sugared paper, carefully removing the tin and its lining. Quickly roll up the cake with the paper inside. Leave overnight.
To assemble the ice cream cake, remove the chocolate and orange ice cream and the sweet peppermint ice cream from the freezer and allow to soften slightly for about 25 minutes at room temperature. Stir the chocolate polka dots into the chocolate and orange ice cream.
Unroll the cake and spread it with the chocolate and orange ice cream. Spoon sweet peppermint ice cream lengthwise down the centre and roll up the cake.
To decorate, spread whipped cream over the cake and sprinkle with grated chocolate. Chill in the freezer for 30 minutes–1 hour before serving.
Serves 6–8

Chocolate meringue and pistachio cake

Metric	Imperial
225 g caster sugar	*8 oz caster sugar*
2 × 15 ml spoons cocoa powder	*2 tablespoons cocoa powder*
4 egg whites	*4 egg whites*
1 quantity Pistachio Ice Cream (page 9)	*1 quantity Pistachio Ice Cream (page 9)*
150 ml double or whipping cream, lightly whipped	*5 fl oz double or whipping cream, lightly whipped*
25 g plain chocolate, grated	*1 oz plain chocolate, grated*
25 g pistachio nuts, skinned and roughly chopped	*1 oz pistachio nuts, skinned and roughly chopped*

Preparation time: 40 minutes, plus cooling and softening
Cooking time: 1¼–1½ hours
Oven: 150°C, 300°F, Gas Mark 2

First make the chocolate meringue. Lightly oil 2 baking trays and cover with lightly oiled greaseproof paper. Sift the caster sugar and the cocoa powder into a bowl. Beat the egg whites until very stiff, then add 2 × 15 ml spoons/2 tablespoons of the cocoa and sugar mixture and beat again for 1 minute. Fold in the remaining cocoa and sugar.
Spoon the mixture into a large forcing bag fitted with a plain 2 cm/¾ inch nozzle and pipe 2 rounds about 20 cm/8 inches in diameter on to the greaseproof paper. Cook in a preheated oven for 1¼–1½ hours until the meringue is set. Carefully peel away the greaseproof paper and leave to go cold.
Remove the pistachio ice cream from the freezer and allow to soften in the refrigerator for 45 minutes. Sandwich the meringue rounds together with the softened ice cream. Spoon the lightly whipped cream over the top and sprinkle with grated chocolate and chopped pistachio nuts. Serve immediately.
Serves 8

Sweet peppermint and chocolate Swiss roll;
Chocolate meringue and pistachio cake

Children's volcano cake

Metric
2 quantities Chocolate and
   Orange Ice Cream
   (page 10)
1 quantity Basic Vanilla
   Ice Cream (page 8)
75 g chocolate polka dots
rind of 1 orange, grated
85 ml Redcurrant Syrup
   (page 24)

Imperial
2 quantities Chocolate and
   Orange Ice Cream
   (page 10)
1 quantity Basic Vanilla
   Ice Cream (page 8)
3 oz chocolate polka dots
rind of 1 orange, grated
3 fl oz Redcurrant Syrup
   (page 24)

Preparation time: 10 minutes, plus softening

Introduce a little fantasy at a children's party with
this quick and amusing method of serving ice cream.
Work as quickly as you can so that the effect of the
cake is not lost as the ice creams melt.

Remove the ice creams from the freezer and allow to
soften in the refrigerator for 45 minutes. Using a large
round serving plate or cake board about 25 cm/10
inches in diameter, scoop or spoon the chocolate and
orange ice cream on to it to form a mound. Top this
with the vanilla ice cream to represent a snow-capped
mountain.
Make a small well in the top of the mountain to form
a crater. Sprinkle chocolate dots over the lower half
of the cake to represent rolling boulders and scatter
grated orange rind over the upper half to represent
falling sparks.
Pour the redcurrant syrup into the crater and allow it
to trickle down the mountain. Serve immediately.
Serves 12

Tropical knickerbocker glory

Metric
½ quantity Mango Ice
   Cream (page 31)
2 Chinese gooseberries,
   peeled and chopped
½ quantity Chinese
   Gooseberry Sorbet
   (page 39)
1 fresh mango, peeled and
   chopped
150 ml Orange Syrup
   (page 24)
120 ml double or whipping
   cream, whipped
25 g flaked almonds,
   toasted

Imperial
½ quantity Mango Ice
   Cream (page 31)
2 Chinese gooseberries,
   peeled and chopped
½ quantity Chinese
   Gooseberry Sorbet
   (page 39)
1 fresh mango, peeled and
   chopped
5 fl oz Orange Syrup
   (page 24)
4 fl oz double or whipping
   cream, whipped
1 oz flaked almonds,
   toasted

Preparation time: 15 minutes, plus softening

This is one suggestion but many combinations of ice
creams and syrups or cold sauces can be tried.

Remove the ice cream and sorbet from the freezer
and allow to soften in the refrigerator for 45 minutes.
Meanwhile, chill 4 large tall glasses in the refrigerator for 15 minutes.
Place a scoop of mango ice cream in the base of each
chilled glass, then sprinkle with a little chopped
Chinese gooseberry. Top with a scoop of Chinese
gooseberry sorbet, then chopped mango. Repeat
this process until the glass is almost full. Pour over
the orange syrup, spoon over the whipped
cream and sprinkle with toasted
almonds. Serve immediately.
Makes 4

Summer fruit knickerbocker glory

Metric
½ quantity Gooseberry Ice Cream (page 37)
½ quantity Raspberry Ice Cream (page 27)
225 g fresh raspberries
150 ml Strawberry Syrup (page 19)
120 ml double or whipping cream, whipped
25 g walnuts, roughly chopped

Imperial
½ quantity Gooseberry Ice Cream (page 37)
½ quantity Raspberry Ice Cream (page 27)
8 oz fresh raspberries
¼ pint Strawberry Syrup (page 19)
4 fl oz double or whipping cream, whipped
1 oz walnuts, roughly chopped

Children's volcano cake; Summer fruit knickerbocker glory; Tropical knickerbocker glory

Preparation time: 15 minutes, plus softening

You can try any combination of ice creams and syrups or cold sauces, instead of those here.

Remove the ice creams from the freezer and allow to soften in the refrigerator for 45 minutes. Meanwhile chill 4 large tall glasses in the refrigerator for 15 minutes.
Fill the chilled glasses with alternate layers of ice cream and fruit, until the glasses are almost full. Pour over the strawberry syrup, top with whipped cream and sprinkle with chopped walnuts. Serve immediately.
Makes 4

BOMBES AND CHARLOTTES

Bombes and charlottes make impressive dinner party sweets, although some patience is required in their preparation. Classic bombe and charlotte moulds are available in most kitchen shops, but if you do not wish to go to the expense of buying these, a plastic or foil bowl may be substituted for a bombe mould, and instead of a charlotte mould a small cake tin may be used. The latter can be tightly covered with cling film, secured with a rubber band and sealed in a freezer bag.

Be sure to measure the liquid capacity of the cake tin before starting to prepare the recipe. The best way to line a bombe mould with ice cream is to use the back of the hand or a wooden spoon.

The ices may be turned out, decorated with cream and returned to the freezer several hours before serving, but to be of a perfect consistency they should be removed from the freezer to the refrigerator approximately 45 minutes before serving.

Rainbow bombe; Almond frascati charlotte

Rainbow bombe

Metric
½ quantity Banana Ice
 Cream (page 30)
½ quantity Gooseberry Ice
 Cream (page 37)
½ quantity Raspberry Ice
 Cream (page 27)
½ quantity Blackberry and
 Apple Ice Cream
 (page 27)

To serve:
150 ml double or whipping
 cream, whipped
few fresh raspberries

Imperial
½ quantity Banana Ice
 Cream (page 30)
½ quantity Gooseberry Ice
 Cream (page 37)
½ quantity Raspberry Ice
 Cream (page 27)
½ quantity Blackberry and
 Apple Ice Cream
 page 27)

To serve:
5 fl oz double or whipping
 cream, whipped
few fresh raspberries

Preparation time: 1 hour, plus overnight chilling, softening and freezing

Chill a 1.2 litre/2 pint bombe mould in the freezer overnight.
Remove the banana ice cream from the freezer and allow to soften slightly for about 25 minutes at room temperature. Use the banana ice cream to cover the base of the bombe mould. Freeze until set.
Repeat this process with each of the three other flavours, chilling before adding the next layer of ice cream. After the final layer, place a circle of oiled greaseproof paper over the ice cream. Cover with the mould lid and freeze for at least 12 hours.
To serve, turn the bombe out on to a plate and decorate with the whipped cream and fresh raspberries. Cut into wedges.
Serves 8

Almond frascati charlotte

Metric
24 Sponge Finger Biscuits
 (page 57)
85 ml coffee liqueur
double or whipping cream,
 whipped, to decorate

**Almond frascati ice
 cream:**
250 ml milk
3 egg yolks
200 g caster sugar
100 g shelled almonds
85 ml water
300 ml double or whipping
 cream, whipped

Imperial
24 Sponge Finger Biscuits
 (page 57)
3 fl oz coffee liqueur
double or whipping cream,
 whipped, to decorate

**Almond frascati ice
 cream:**
8 fl oz milk
3 egg yolks
8 oz caster sugar
4 oz shelled almonds
3 fl oz water
10 fl oz double or whipping
 cream, whipped

Preparation time: 45 minutes, plus freezing
Cooking time: 30 minutes

To make the almond frascati ice cream, gently heat the milk in a heavy-based saucepan. Whisk the egg yolks and 100 g/4 oz of the sugar together until thick and pale. Gradually pour the hot milk over the yolk mixture, stirring constantly. Pour the mixture back into the saucepan and stir over a gentle heat until thick enough to coat the back of a wooden spoon. Do not boil. Pour the custard into a bowl to go cold.
Rinse the almonds to remove any dust from·the skins. Put the water and the remaining sugar into a heavy-based saucepan and heat gently until the sugar has dissolved. Add the almonds, increase the heat and boil for about 10 minutes until golden brown and syrupy. Pour into an oiled baking tin to set.
When cold, pulverize the almond mixture on a chopping board, using a clean cloth and a rolling pin. Alternatively use a coffee grinder. Stir all but 1 × 15 ml spoon/1 tablespoon of the finely ground praline into the custard with the whipped cream. Pour into a freezer container and freeze for 3–4 hours. Beat the mixture twice, at hourly intervals during this time.
Cover the base of a charlotte mould with oiled grease-proof paper. Lightly brush the sponge finger biscuits with a little of the coffee liqueur and use them to line the sides of the mould. Break the remaining sponge fingers into small pieces in a bowl with the rest of the liqueur to soak.
Spoon half of the almond frascati ice cream into the lined mould and cover with a layer of the soaked sponge fingers. Spoon over the remaining ice cream. Cover, seal and freeze for at least 12 hours.
To serve, turn the charlotte out and decorate with whipped cream and the reserved praline.
Serves 8

Coffee and sultana charlotte

Metric
16 Sponge Finger Biscuits
  (page 57)

**Coffee and sultana ice
  cream:**
450 ml milk
1 × 15 ml spoon freshly
  ground, or instant,
  strong coffee
4 egg yolks
75 g caster sugar
75 g sultanas, soaked
  overnight in 2 × 15 ml
  spoons brandy
150 ml double or whipping
  cream, whipped

To decorate:
300 ml double or whipping
  cream, whipped
24 baby meringues
grated mocha or plain
  chocolate

Imperial
16 Sponge Finger Biscuits
  (page 57)

**Coffee and sultana ice
  cream:**
¾ pint milk
1 tablespoon freshly
  ground, or instant,
  strong coffee
4 egg yolks
3 oz caster sugar
3 oz sultanas, soaked
  overnight in 2
  tablespoons brandy
5 fl oz double or whipping
  cream, whipped

To decorate:
10 fl oz double or whipping
  cream, whipped
24 baby meringues
grated mocha or plain
  chocolate

Preparation time: 1 hour, plus overnight soaking, and freezing
Cooking time: about 25 minutes

To make the ice cream, bring the milk and coffee slowly to the boil in a heavy-based saucepan. Remove from the heat, cover and, if using fresh coffee, leave to infuse for 10 minutes. Strain through a fine nylon strainer, then return the mixture to the saucepan and heat gently until warm.
Whisk the egg yolks and sugar in a large bowl until thick and pale. Gradually pour the warm milk over the yolk mixture, stirring constantly. Pour the mixture back into the saucepan, and stir over a gentle heat until the custard thickens enough to coat the back of a wooden spoon. Do not allow to boil. Cool, then pour into a freezer container and freeze for about 1½ hours until mushy.
Fold in the sultanas in brandy and the whipped cream, then freeze for at least 1½–2 hours, until firm. Beat the mixture twice during this time.
Cover the base of a charlotte mould with oiled greaseproof paper and line the sides with the sponge finger biscuits. Spoon the ice cream into the centre. Cover, seal and freeze for at least 12 hours.
To serve, turn the charlotte out on to a plate and decorate with whipped cream, meringues and grated chocolate. Cut into wedges.
Serves 8

Chocolate and almond charlotte

Metric
16 Sponge Finger Biscuits
  (page 57)

**Chocolate and almond
  ice cream:**
450 ml single cream
50 g ground almonds
3 egg yolks
100 g caster sugar
75 g plain chocolate,
  melted
75 g flaked almonds,
  toasted
250 ml double or whipping
  cream, whipped
3 × 15 ml spoons orange
  liqueur

To decorate:
double or whipping cream,
  whipped
crystallized violet petals

Imperial
16 Sponge Finger Biscuits
  (page 57)

**Chocolate and almond
  ice cream:**
15 fl oz single cream
2 oz ground almonds
3 egg yolks
4 oz caster sugar
3 oz plain chocolate,
  melted
3 oz flaked almonds,
  toasted
8 fl oz double or whipping
  cream, whipped
3 tablespoons orange
  liqueur

To decorate:
double or whipping cream,
  whipped
crystallized violet petals

Preparation time: 1 hour, plus freezing
Cooking time: about 25 minutes

To make the ice cream, gently heat the single cream with the ground almonds in a heavy-based saucepan. Whisk the egg yolks and sugar together until thick and pale. Gradually pour the hot cream mixture over the yolks and sugar, stirring constantly.
Pour the mixture back into the saucepan and stir over a gentle heat until the custard thickens enough to coat the back of a wooden spoon. Do not allow to boil. Remove from the heat and stir in the melted chocolate. Pour into a freezer container and freeze for about 1½ hours until the mixture is mushy.
Fold in the flaked almonds, whipped cream and orange liqueur, then freeze for at least 1½–2 hours, until firm. Beat the mixture twice during this time.
Cover the base of a charlotte mould with oiled greaseproof paper and line the sides with the sponge finger biscuits. Spoon the ice cream into the centre. Cover, seal and freeze for at least 12 hours.
To serve, turn the charlotte out on to a plate and decorate with whipped cream and crystallized violet petals. Cut into wedges.
Serves 8

Top shelf: Chocolate and almond charlotte
Bottom shelf: Coffee and sultana charlotte

Brown breadcrumb and violet bombe

Metric

1 quantity Brown
Breadcrumb Ice Cream
(page 14)

Violet mousse:

4 × 15 ml spoons water
75 g caster sugar
4 egg yolks
25 g crystallized violet
petals
3 × 15 ml spoons orange
liqueur
450 ml double or whipping
cream, whipped

To decorate:

150 ml double or whipping
cream
crystallized violet petals
25 g breadcrumbs, toasted

Imperial

1 quantity Brown
Breadcrumb Ice Cream
(page 14)

Violet mousse:

4 tablespoons water
3 oz caster sugar
4 egg yolks
1 oz crystallized violet
petals
3 tablespoons orange
liqueur
15 fl oz double or whipping
cream, whipped

To decorate:

5 fl oz double or whipping
cream
crystallized violet petals
1 oz breadcrumbs, toasted

Preparation time: 45 minutes, plus overnight chilling, softening and freezing
Cooking time: 15 minutes

Chill a 1.2 litre/2 pint bombe mould in the freezer overnight.

Remove the brown breadcrumb ice cream from the freezer and allow to soften slightly for about 25 minutes at room temperature. Completely line the chilled mould with the brown breadcrumb ice cream and return it to the freezer for at least 30 minutes.

To make the violet mousse, pour the water into a heavy-based saucepan and stir in the sugar. Heat gently, stirring all the time, until the sugar has dissolved. Increase the heat and cook rapidly until the thread stage is reached (see page 6). Cool.

Beat the egg yolks with an electric mixer until pale and doubled in volume. Gradually beat in the syrup and fold in the violet petals, liqueur and cream.

Spoon the mousse into the lined mould, cover with an oiled circle of greaseproof paper and the mould lid. Freeze for at least 12 hours.

To serve, turn the bombe out on to a plate, decorate with whipped cream and crystallized violet petals, and sprinkle with toasted breadcrumbs. Cut into wedges.

Serves 8

Hazelnut surprise bombe

Metric
450 ml single cream
3 egg yolks
100 g caster sugar
50 g hazelnuts, finely
  chopped and toasted
150 ml double or whipping
  cream, whipped

Imperial
15 fl oz single cream
3 egg yolks
4 oz caster sugar
2 oz hazelnuts, finely
  chopped and toasted
5 fl oz double or whipping
  cream, whipped

Chocolate mousse:
4 × 15 ml spoons water
75 g caster sugar
4 egg yolks
75 g plain chocolate,
  melted
350 ml double or whipping
  cream, whipped
3 × 15 ml spoons coffee
  liqueur
50 g whole hazelnuts,
  toasted

Chocolate mousse:
4 tablespoons water
3 oz caster sugar
4 egg yolks
3 oz plain chocolate,
  melted
12 fl oz double or whipping
  cream, whipped
3 tablespoons coffee
  liqueur
2 oz whole hazelnuts,
  toasted

To decorate:
300 ml double or whipping
  cream, whipped
whole hazelnuts
chocolate polka dots

To decorate:
10 fl oz double or whipping
  cream, whipped
whole hazelnuts
chocolate polka dots

Preparation time: 1 hour, plus overnight chilling, and freezing
Cooking time: 30 minutes

Chill a 1.2 litre/2 pint bombe mould in the freezer overnight.
To make a hazelnut ice cream, gently heat the single cream in a heavy-based saucepan. Beat the egg yolks and sugar together in a large bowl until thick and pale yellow in colour. Gradually pour the hot cream into the egg mixture, stirring all the time. Pour the mixture back into the saucepan, and stir over a gentle heat until the custard thickens enough to coat the back of a wooden spoon. Do not boil. Allow to cool.
Fold the chopped toasted hazelnuts and whipped cream into the custard. Pour the mixture into a freezer container and freeze for 2–3 hours until frozen softly, beating twice during the freezing process. Line the bombe mould with the hazelnut ice cream and return it to the freezer.
To make the chocolate mousse, pour the water into a heavy-based saucepan and stir in the sugar. Heat gently until the sugar has dissolved. Increase the heat and cook rapidly until the thread stage is reached (see page 6). Allow to cool.
Beat the egg yolks with an electric mixer until pale and doubled in volume. Gradually beat in the syrup. Stir in the melted chocolate and fold in the whipped cream, coffee liqueur and whole toasted hazelnuts.
Spoon the mousse into the centre of the bombe mould. Cover with an oiled circle of greaseproof paper and the mould lid. Freeze for at least 12 hours.
To serve, turn the bombe out on to a plate and decorate with whipped cream, hazelnuts and chocolate polka dots. Cut into wedges.
Serves 8

From left: Brown breadcrumb and violet bombe; Hazelnut surprise bombe

Ginger ice cream and biscuit bombe

Metric
*1 quantity Ginger Ice
 Cream (page 15)*
*215 g ginger or digestive
 biscuits*
*150 ml double or whipping
 cream, whipped*

Imperial
*1 quantity Ginger Ice
 Cream (page 15)*
*7½ oz ginger or digestive
 biscuits*
*5 fl oz double or whipping
 cream, whipped*

Preparation time: about 45 minutes, plus softening and freezing

Remove the ginger ice cream from the freezer and allow to soften slightly for about 25 minutes at room temperature. Place the biscuits in a plastic bag and crush them with a rolling pin.

Lightly oil the base and sides of a bombe mould. Place a strip of greaseproof paper across the base and up opposite sides, leaving short handles above the edge of the mould.

Spoon enough ginger ice cream into the base of the mould to form a thin layer, then sprinkle with a few of the crushed biscuits. Fill with alternate layers of ice cream and crushed biscuits until full, finishing with a layer of biscuits. Cover with oiled greaseproof paper and the mould lid. Freeze for at least 12 hours. To remove the bombe from the mould, gently ease the greaseproof paper handles and invert the bombe on to a plate.

To serve, pipe with rosettes of whipped cream. Cut into wedges.

Serves 8

Passion fruit and peach bombe

Metric
1 quantity Passion Fruit
 Ice Cream (page 31)
2 fresh passion fruit, to
 decorate

Peach mousse:
4 × 15 ml spoons water
75 g caster sugar
4 egg yolks
3 ripe peaches, peeled,
 stoned and coarsely
 chopped
250 ml double or whipping
 cream, whipped
2 × 15 ml spoons orange
 liqueur

Imperial
1 quantity Passion Fruit
 Ice Cream (page 31)
2 fresh passion fruit, to
 decorate

Peach mousse:
4 tablespoons water
3 oz caster sugar
4 egg yolks
3 ripe peaches, peeled,
 stoned and coarsely
 chopped
8 fl oz double or whipping
 cream, whipped
2 tablespoons orange
 liqueur

Preparation time: 45 minutes, plus overnight chilling, softening and freezing
Cooking time: 15 minutes

Chill a 1.2 litre/2 pint bombe mould overnight in the freezer.
Remove the passion fruit ice cream from the freezer and allow to soften slightly for about 25 minutes at room temperature. Completely line the chilled mould with a layer of the passion fruit ice cream and return it to the freezer for at least 30 minutes.
To make the peach mousse, pour the water into a heavy-based saucepan and add the sugar. Heat gently until the sugar has dissolved. Increase the heat and cook rapidly until the thread stage is reached (page 6). Allow to cool.
Beat the egg yolks with an electric mixer until pale and double in volume. Gradually beat in the syrup. Fold the chopped peaches into the yolk mixture with the whipped cream and the orange liqueur.
Spoon the mousse into the lined mould, cover the base with an oiled circle of greaseproof paper and the mould lid. Freeze for at least 12 hours.
To serve, turn the bombe out on to a plate. Using a small spoon scoop out the flesh from the fresh passion fruit and arrange over the bombe. Cut into wedges.
Serves 8

Vanilla and strawberry bombe

Metric
1 quantity Vanilla Ice
 Cream (page 8)

Strawberry mousse:
4 × 15 ml spoons water
75 g caster sugar
4 egg yolks
150 ml double or whipping
 cream, whipped
225 g fresh strawberries,
 puréed
2 × 15 ml spoons orange
 liqueur

To decorate:
300 ml double or whipping
 cream
1 × 15 ml spoon orange
 liqueur
small fresh strawberries
crystallized rose petals

Imperial
1 quantity Vanilla Ice
 Cream (page 8)

Strawberry mousse:
4 tablespoons water
3 oz caster sugar
4 egg yolks
5 fl oz double or whipping
 cream, whipped
8 oz fresh strawberries,
 puréed
2 tablespoons orange
 liqueur

To decorate:
10 fl oz double or whipping
 cream
1 tablespoon orange
 liqueur
small fresh strawberries
crystallized rose petals

Preparation time: 45 minutes, plus overnight chilling, softening and freezing
Cooking time: 15 minutes

Chill a 1.2 litre/2 pint bombe mould in the freezer overnight.
Remove the vanilla ice cream from the freezer and allow to soften slightly for about 25 minutes at room temperature. Completely line the chilled mould with a layer of vanilla ice cream, reserving sufficient to cover the top of the mould later. Return the mould and the remaining vanilla ice cream to the freezer.
To make the strawberry mousse, pour the water into a heavy-based saucepan and add the sugar. Heat gently until the sugar has dissolved. Increase the heat and cook rapidly until the thread stage is reached (see page 6). Allow to cool.
Beat the egg yolks with an electric mixer until pale and doubled in volume. Gradually beat in the syrup. Fold the whipped cream and the strawberry purée into the mixture and add the orange liqueur.
Spoon the mousse into the lined mould, leaving a gap of about 5 mm/¼ inch at the top. Fill this gap with the remaining vanilla ice cream. Cover with an oiled circle of greaseproof paper and the mould lid. Freeze for at least 12 hours.
To serve, whip the cream and fold in the orange liqueur. Turn the bombe out on to a plate. Pipe with rosettes of cream and decorate with fresh strawberries and crystallized rose petals. Cut into wedges.
Serves 8

From left: Ginger ice cream and biscuit bombe; Vanilla and strawberry bombe; Passion fruit and peach bombe

INDEX